PUT IT IN WRITING

Context, text and language

Joanne Rossbridge with Kathy Rushton

Preface by Beverly Derewianka

PETAA
PRIMARY ENGLISH TEACHING
ASSOCIATION AUSTRALIA

Published 2015
Primary English Teaching Association Australia (PETAA)
Laura St, Newtown, NSW 2042, Australia
PO Box 3106, Marrickville Metro, NSW 2204
Ph: (02) 8020 3900
Fax: (02) 8020 3933
Email: info@petaa.edu.au
Website: www.petaa.edu.au

ISBN: 978-1-925132-21-2 (Printed edn)
ISBN: 978-1-925132-22-9 (ePub edn)

National Library of Australia Cataloguing-in-Publication entry
Author: Rossbridge, Joanne, author.
Title: Put it in writing: context, text and language / Joanne Rossbridge (author); Kathy Rushton (contributor).
ISBN: 9781925132212 (paperback)
Notes: Includes bibliographical references.
Subjects: Language arts (Primary)–Australia. English language–Written English–Study and teaching (Primary)–Australia.
English language–Composition and exercises–Study and teaching (Primary)–Australia.
Other Authors/Contributors: Rushton, Kathleen, 1950- contributor. Primary English Teaching Association (Australia)
Dewey Number: 372.623044

Cover and text design by Nice Stuff
Illustrations by Nice Stuff
Edited and project managed by Rema Gnanadickam, Zodiac Publishing Services
Printed in Australia by Finsbury Green

PETAA
PRIMARY ENGLISH TEACHING
ASSOCIATION AUSTRALIA

Contents

Acknowledgements

The authors and publisher gratefully acknowledge the use of the following copyright material in this publication.

Walker Books, London, for permission to reproduce the text extract and images from *Don't Let the pigeon drive the bus!* by Mo Willems on pages **19–20**, **22**, **23** and **28**; Duck Duck Moose Inc for ChatterPix Kids images reproduced on pages **26** and **27**; Walker Books Australia for permission to reproduce from *Silver Buttons* by Bob Graham text extract on pages **34–35** and images on pages **31**, **33** and **39**; iStock images for permission to reproduce photograph on page **41**; Penguin Books Australia for permission to reproduce from *Blueback* by Tim Winton text extracts on pages **47–48** and book cover on page **44**; Middle Harbour Public School for permission to reproduce images of student work samples on pages **52** and **53**; Dorling Kindersley Ltd for permission to reproduce images from *101 great science experiments* on page **60**; Wordle.net for Wordle work sample on page **67**; Australian Academy for Science for permission to reproduce text extract from Primary Connections on page **68**; eHow.com for permission to reproduce text on Amazon and Daintree rainforests on page **76**; Allen & Unwin for permission to reproduce text and cover image from *Australians all* by Nadia Wheatley on pages **88**, **91** and **129**; Matchbox Pictures, Producer Penny Chapman, for permission to reproduce still from 'First contact, My Place video First contact Episode 24, 1788: Dan' on page **94**; LittleHare Books, an imprint of Hardie Grant Egmont, for permission to reproduce text extract and images from *Parachute* by Danny Parker and Matt Ottley on pages **104**, **106–107**, **109**.

While every effort has been made to trace and acknowledge copyright and ownership of all included works, should any infringement has occurred, the publisher offers their apologies and invite copyright owners to contact them.

Preface

Put it in writing provides a very practical and engaging guide to teaching students to successfully meet the writing demands of the Australian Curriculum.

Joanne Rossbridge and Kathy Rushton build on a long tradition of teaching writing from a functional perspective. Some thirty years ago, Australia saw the beginnings of a fresh way of looking at language and literacy, inspired by the work of Professor Michael Halliday. Research had shown that primary students were writing a very limited range of texts – primarily recounts of personal experience (eg, Martin 1985; Rothery 1996; Christie & Martin 1997). Researchers set about examining the various purposes for which students needed to use language across the different areas of the curriculum, identifying a number of key genres such as procedures, narratives, explanations, information reports, recounts and arguments. Drawing on such research, in 1990 PETAA (then PETA) published what came to be known as 'the pink book', *Exploring how texts work*, making the findings available to classroom practitioners.

In the years between then and now, genre theory has continued to evolve and *Put it in writing* reflects these developments. From the basic half dozen genres canvassed in *Exploring how texts work*, further investigation has distinguished a much more detailed array of genre families. Recounts, for example, might include recounting what happened in a science experiment, or recounting an episode from history, or recounting the events in a person's life, or recounting a sequence from an imaginary or literary perspective.

While early versions of genre theory described how different genres unfold in characteristic broad stages, *Put it in writing* picks up on more recent developments, recognising that within each stage we can identify minor phases. Within the orientation stage of a narrative, for example, we might find phases introducing the characters, or establishing the setting and mood, or describing an initiating event, or giving a flashback. While the stages are relatively obligatory to the success of the genre, the phases provide an element of flexibility: there is a choice as to whether to include them or not and in which order – or even to insert unexpected phases or phases that respond to a particular task. *Put it in writing*, for example, describes how *Don't let the pigeon drive the bus!* includes phases of interaction between the pigeon and the reader, phases of reaction by the pigeon, and phases of internal reflection.

By considering the phases in a text, we are better able to identify the language choices typical of the phase and therefore to determine a potential focus for teaching. An interaction phase in a narrative, for example, will generally involve dialogue: choice of saying verb (usually in past tense), use of direct speech (including appropriate punctuation), speech functions such as questions, statements and commands, an indication of how something is said (eg, *in a nasty snarl*), and so on.

Put it in writing also reflects recent advances in genre theory regarding multimodal texts, as outlined in Jon Callow's recent PETAA publication, *The shape of texts to come.* Genre theory provides a set of tools for analysing images (still and moving) and the relationship between images and written text. In relation to *Silver Buttons*, for example, Rossbridge and Rushton introduce students to notions such as shot distance and how visual features function in relation to verbal text.

Another recent development in genre theory is an examination of how language is used interpersonally to express attitudes: sharing feelings and opinions, evaluating the qualities of things, and judging human behaviour. These resources are explored in historical recounts from *Australians all* in terms of how individuals and groups of people are named and the cultural and historical significance.

Put it in writing is a welcome and timely contribution to the teaching of writing, embodying the principles associated with a functional approach: a view of language as a system of choices; a model of language in context; and a commitment to equity so that all students are supported to achieve learning outcomes through explicit teaching.

Beverly Derewianka
Professorial Fellow
University of Wollongong

Put it in writing: Context, text and language

The development of this book was inspired by the ground breaking work of Beverly Derewianka who wrote *Exploring how texts work* (1990) which gave primary teachers the tools for working with genres in their classrooms. The influence of her work, with its focus on the purpose, structure and language features of a range of texts, has meant that many teachers now have the language to talk explicitly about texts in their classrooms. The aim of *Put it in writing* is to build upon that work and provide models, guides and processes to help teachers and their students give serious and careful thought to the texts they are reading and writing. In expanding upon the contribution of *Exploring how texts work*, this book investigates a range of genres across curriculum areas. It incorporates the notion of stages with the flexibility of phases for looking at text structure when engaging with multimodal and visual texts. In addition, it further draws on a functional approach to language including more recent developments based on appraisal theory. In doing so, knowledge and processes for implementing the Australian Curriculum are supported.

This book offers models to support the teaching of writing and is organised around the strands of knowledge about texts and language and support for the learner. These aspects are interrelated (Figure 1), as having knowledge about text and language is not sufficient unless it can be transferred into pedagogical knowledge (Myhill, Jones & Watson, 2013). The ideas in this introduction provide the framework within which we have selected and analysed texts and provided practical teaching examples.

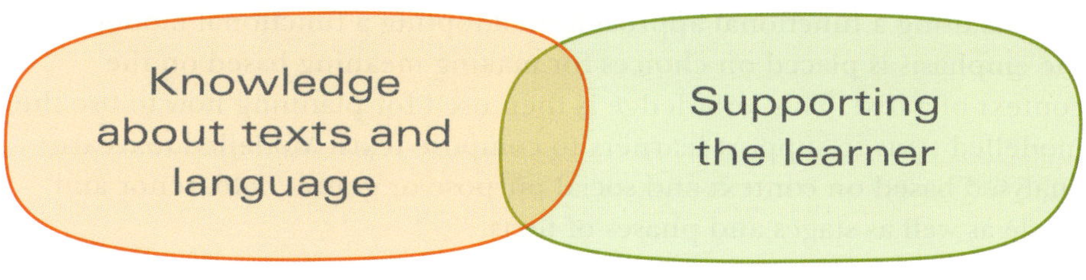

Figure 1 Interrelationship between knowledge about texts and supporting the learner

Knowledge about texts and language

The *Australian Curriculum: English* acknowledges the importance of knowledge about texts and language, with 'Language: knowing about the English language' (ACARA, 2012), being one of the three interrelated strands organising the content. Knowing about texts and language requires knowledge of how language works to make meaning. Providing students with such knowledge gives them both access to and makes explicit, the valued texts found in schooling. A functional approach to language including genre theory (Halliday & Hasan, 1985, Christie, 2005, Martin & Rose, 2012, Derewianka & Jones, 2012) underpins the development of knowledge about language and how it works.

Teacher knowledge is critical for supporting students to write texts using a variety of language modes. An understanding of a functional model of language and genre theory ensures teachers are equipped to explicitly support students with metalanguage that can enable students to talk about the language choices in texts composed across curriculum contexts. Talk and reflection based on language as a system of meanings has been seen to improve student writing (Williams, 2005; Myhill, Jones & Watson, 2013b). The *Australian Curriculum: English* (2015) supports this approach stating:

> By developing a body of knowledge about these patterns and their connections, students learn to communicate effectively through coherent, well-structured sentences and texts. They gain a consistent way of understanding and talking about language, language-in-use and language-as-system, so they can reflect on their own speaking and writing and discuss these productively with others.

A functional model

In each section of this book models are provided to show how teacher knowledge about texts and language is developed through an analysis of texts using a functional approach. In adopting a functional model the emphasis is placed on choices for making meaning based on the context of a text. This knowledge is then used for planning how to use the modelled texts to support learners to compose texts. Modelled texts are analysed based on context and social purpose or genre, field, tenor and mode as well as stages and phases of texts.

Context

Meanings and choices in texts are determined by the social, cultural and historical factors underlying the situational and broader cultural context. In schooling this is important, as particular texts are valued in the educational context and in different subject areas. Spoken and written language as well as visual choices may differ depending on the context.

Social purpose/genre

The cultural context of a text relates to the discourse in which it is situated. In this book it is educational discourse which is valued. Within this cultural context there are a variety of purposes for using language such as narrating a fairytale in English, recounting experiments in Science, or persuading an audience to a way of thinking about historical events in History. These are referred to as genres (or sometimes text types or types of texts). Much research has been conducted on the teaching of genres in schools (Christie & Derewianka, 2008). To identify the genre of a text the social purpose needs to be identified – to explain, to instruct, to describe, etc. The genre is a way of achieving the social purpose with the social purpose reflecting the overall goal of the text.

A genre has a typical text structure that unfolds across the text to achieve its social purpose. Focusing only on the stages or text structure of a text is problematic as it is too simplistic and potentially formulaic. Often the genre of a text may seem problematic as sometimes texts may have multiple purposes depending on their contexts. These are sometimes referred to as hybrid texts or 'macrogenres'.

The *Australian Curriculum: English* places texts into three broad categories: imaginative, informative and persuasive. The three sections in this book have been organised around these broad purposes for using language (Figure 2).

Figure 2
Categories of texts

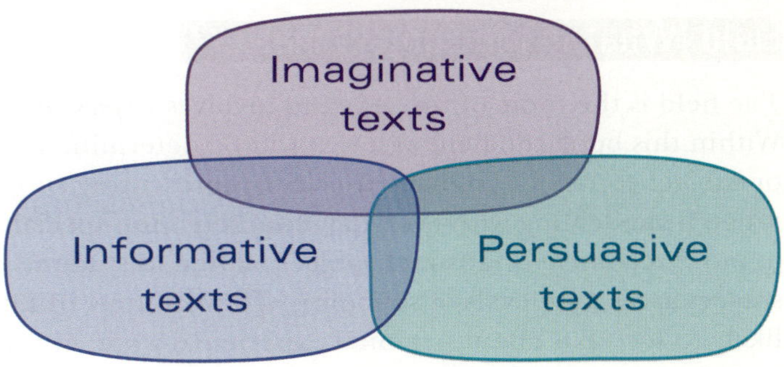

In working with these categories teachers can draw on the significant work of the genre movement to consider the context and articulate the purposes and features of particular texts. A text may be categorised as informative, however its purpose needs to be discussed explicitly and in context as, for example, informative texts can achieve a range of purposes. These can range from instructing and recounting to describing and explaining. Due to the complex function of some texts, they may fit into more than one of these categories and may have multiple purposes.

The register of a text is the relationship between the text and its context. The main factors in the context are the field (subject matter), tenor (roles and relationships) and mode (channel of communication). This is reflected in the *Australian Curriculum: English* (ACARA, 2012):

> English uses standard grammatical terminology within a contextual framework, in which language choices are seen to vary according to the **topics at hand**, the nature and proximity of **the relationships between the language users**, and the **modalities or channels of communication** available.

The three key substrands in the Language strand in the *Australian Curriculum: English* have been developed on an understanding of register. They are: *Expressing and developing ideas*; *Language for interaction*; *Text structure and organisation* reflecting concepts of field, tenor, and mode.

When working with texts, it is strongly recommended that teachers are familiar with the relationship between context (genre and register) and the choices made in creating a text. The social purpose and genre of a text determine the overall structure, while combinations of the register variables of field, tenor and mode influence the language choices in a particular situation. These understandings are key to developing students' resources for making choices when writing. For this reason the field, tenor and mode of each modelled text has also been analysed within the models across the book.

Field (What is the subject matter?)

The field is the topic of the text and involves *Expressing and developing ideas*. Within this book the field of a text will be determined by the curriculum or subject context. Language used for representing subject matter may range from dealing with everyday, concrete, non-specialised subject matter to more technical or abstract subject matter, as students move between subject areas and levels of schooling. For example, in English we are more likely to see texts about personal experience while in Science a text may be technical such as when writing about natural phenomena.

Tenor (Who is involved and what is the relationship?)

The tenor of a text is related to the roles and relationships when *Interacting with others.* Tenor can be influenced by factors such as age, gender, social status, expertise etc. Choices will also be reflected by the nature of contact between participants such as the familiarity, frequency and feelings of those involved. In school contexts, students are often required to write as experts for an audience they never have nor will ever meet, particularly as writing becomes more academic in nature. When working with students we can consider engagement with the audience through the adoption of points of view, the expression of opinions, sharing of feelings and the judgement of behaviour.

Mode (What is the channel of communication?)

The mode of a text refers to the organisational features for creating cohesive texts through *Text structure and organisation* and reflects discourse which may range from spoken to written-like language. The mode may range from spoken-like, spontaneous texts to more dense, written-like, planned and carefully crafted texts often valued at school. The mode of a text may also be visual or a combination of visual and verbal text. Due to the contextual influences on texts, particularly with regard to technology in recent times, choices made in representing meanings in various modes should be considered (Callow, 2013). Texts have become more multimodal in nature than the genres or text types first identified as critical to schooling success (Martin & Rose, 2008). For this reason it is all the more important to look at the choices made in texts within context.

Text structure and phases

By developing talk and knowledge about texts at the level of context, genre and register, choices at the text structure level can be considered in more critical and purposeful ways. For example, the typical stages of a narrative are often described as orientation, complication and resolution. However, when looking at less traditional contexts and forms we may see variation in such stages. Within the stages of a text, phases can be identified and described in greater detail in terms of the role they are performing within the stages. 'Stages are the relatively broad stretches of text that are characteristic of most texts belonging to a particular genre. The phases are much more flexible and vary from text to text, depending on the particular topic or audience' (Derewianka & Jones, 2012, p. 116).

Again, if taking the narrative example, phases such as description of a setting and introduction of characters may occur at the beginning of a narrative. Alternatively events and a character's reaction could be phases that a writer draws upon in order to achieve that stage of the text.

Using modelled texts to develop metalanguage

When interacting with texts in context it becomes clear that a metalanguage for talking about texts is required. To acknowledge the relationship between form and function both traditional and functional terms will be used throughout the book, as there is an emphasis on talking about language use in context, and in particular, choices available when writing texts. Much conversation occurs at the group level when considering *Expressing and connecting ideas.* Noun groups will be described as naming the participants in a text; verb groups represent the processes in which the participants are involved and adverbials tell about the circumstantial detail surrounding the actions such as where, when and how. When considering *Interacting with others,* resources for discussing evaluation and attitude are drawn upon as well as the use of speech functions to show roles and relationships between a writer and audience. Discussion of *Text structure and organisation* uses resources for considering aspects of cohesion such as connectives and word associations, or chains across texts. By developing a shared metalanguage to explore the relationship between context and text, the classroom becomes a place of reflection and critical analysis of language choices.

For further detail on the grammar required for developing a shared metalanguage it is suggested that this book be read with reference to *A new grammar companion* (Derewianka, 2011) and *Grammar and meaning* (Humphrey, Droga & Feez, 2012). As indicated by Humphrey, Droga and Feez (2012), talk about language as a system requires a 'toolkit'. This can be shared between students and teachers and fostered in classrooms with conversations initiated, developed and extended around contexts, texts and their features. When students respond to the texts of others by drawing on a toolkit they can then reflect on their own texts and are better able to develop and enhance their own compositions.

Figure 3 demonstrates how the field, tenor and mode are expressed through language choices. This includes potential metalanguage for discussing both verbal and visual choices made across modes of texts and conceptualises grammar as a descriptive tool for depicting how language works in context. The functional model involves discussion and reflection on language choices which sets up a particular pedagogy placing the focus on pedagogical tools rather than just teaching grammar discretely and out of context (Myhill, Jones, Watson & Lines, 2013).

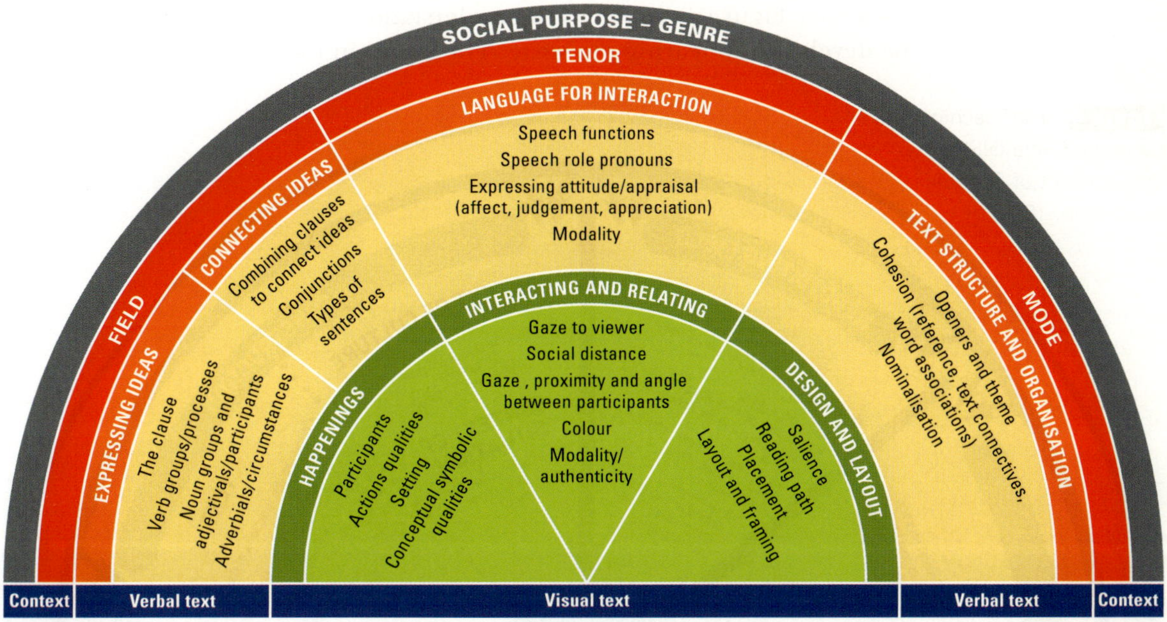

Figure 3 Connecting context to language choices in verbal and visual texts (Adapted from Derewianka 2011; Humphrey, Droga & Feez 2012; Callow, 2013)

Supporting the learner

To teach writing successfully, careful planning decisions need to be made based on the analysis of the features of texts students will write and consequently the selection of appropriate models for writing. From this strong foundation, teaching and learning sequences can be developed which will effectively support learners. The models in this book have used the teaching and learning cycle to design teaching sequences with a spotlight or focus on a particular stage in the cycle provided within each model.

The teaching and learning cycle

The 'Teaching and Learning Cycle', sometimes known as 'The Curriculum Cycle' was developed by the Sydney School genre theorists working with teachers in the Metropolitan East Region of Sydney's Disadvantaged Schools Program in the 1980s (Humphrey & Macnaught, 2011). The cycle (see Figure 4) supports the understandings and skills that need to be developed in learning to write. The stages in the cycle are negotiating

Figure 4 The Teaching and Learning Cycle (NSW Department of School Education, 1992)

or building the field, deconstructing text and jointly and independently constructing text. The purpose of the cycle is to scaffold students as they move from high support to the need for less support and as they develop control of subject matter and language choices in the written mode. The focus on handing control over to the students at the site of the 'Zone of Proximal Development' (Vygotsky & Kozulin, 1986) is evident as teachers continually monitor the support needed during the teaching cycle as they move back and forth through stages of the cycle based on student need. The cycle is a form of macro scaffolding (Hammond, 2001) as teachers consider support through the planning, designing and sequencing of teaching strategies. At the micro level further scaffolding is provided as teachers and students interact around texts in context, their subject matter and particularly their language features.

Building the field

Before considering writing, students need to become acquainted with the subject matter as well as the discourse of the subject. This may involve undertaking a range of experiences and engaging with a variety of texts. Building the field must obviously start before writing begins but it is an ongoing process that develops as students read, write and talk about the subject and refine ways to express their ideas. This process continues during text deconstruction, joint construction and preparation for independent construction. Throughout this book we have used an adaptation of the teaching and learning cycle to show how field is continually built during all phases of text composition (Figure 5).

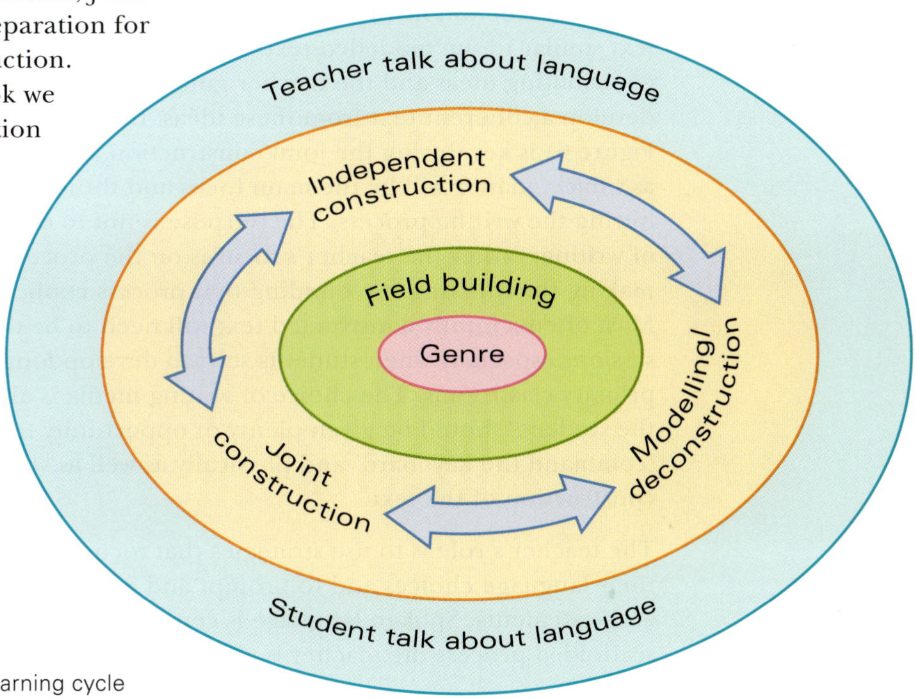

Figure 5
Adapted teaching and learning cycle

Text deconstruction/modelled reading

During the deconstruction stage the teacher guides the students to identify the purpose of the text and how the stages and phases of the text help achieve the purpose. Additionally, language features are discussed which are relevant to the field, tenor or the mode rather than just the field or subject matter only. The preparation and selection of texts at the point of deconstruction has a significant impact upon the teacher-guided conversation during joint construction. Metalanguage and critical literacy can only be developed if there is something interesting to discuss. So, the modelled text must be rich, relevant and engaging. It is important to choose texts that will show appropriate language choices for the purpose and genre. Such texts should build students' knowledge at all levels of text – from whole text, to paragraph, sentence, group and word level (Derewianka, 2011, p. 11). It is important to note that the texts engaged with when reading to build the field will differ to the texts chosen for deconstruction, as the latter will be based on the genre and not necessarily the subject matter. In some of the examples in this book texts have been selected in order to build the field while in others they are based on the genre students are required to write.

Joint construction

Joint construction involves the teacher and students jointly constructing a text similar to the modelled text. There is a balance between the students contributing ideas and the teacher guiding or demonstrating how to develop a coherent text from these ideas. Interactive discussion (see Figure 6) is key during the joint construction as language choices as well as subject matter will be the main focus and these need to be evaluated during the writing process. The purpose is not to develop a finished piece of writing; rather the teacher's focus is on the process of writing and on making the thinking surrounding that process explicit and transparent. Most often a jointly constructed text will need to be developed over several sessions especially when students start to develop longer texts in upper primary classrooms. The choice of writing media is also important, as the students should be given plenty of opportunity to 'share the pen' or 'command the keyboard' and physically as well as verbally share in the construction of the text.

The teacher's role is to use strategies that focus the students' attention on their language choices and to prompt and guide them through questions and statements. Spoken language is central to the activity and in this scaffolded process the teacher is able to both challenge and support the students (Hammond, 2001). Through paraphrasing and recasting (Gibbons, 2002) the teacher is able to provide the support that is needed at the point of learning. The joint construction provides maximum support in a guided experience that helps individual students to make informed decisions about all aspects of writing from text structure, punctuation and spelling to choices at the level of clause, sentence and paragraph.

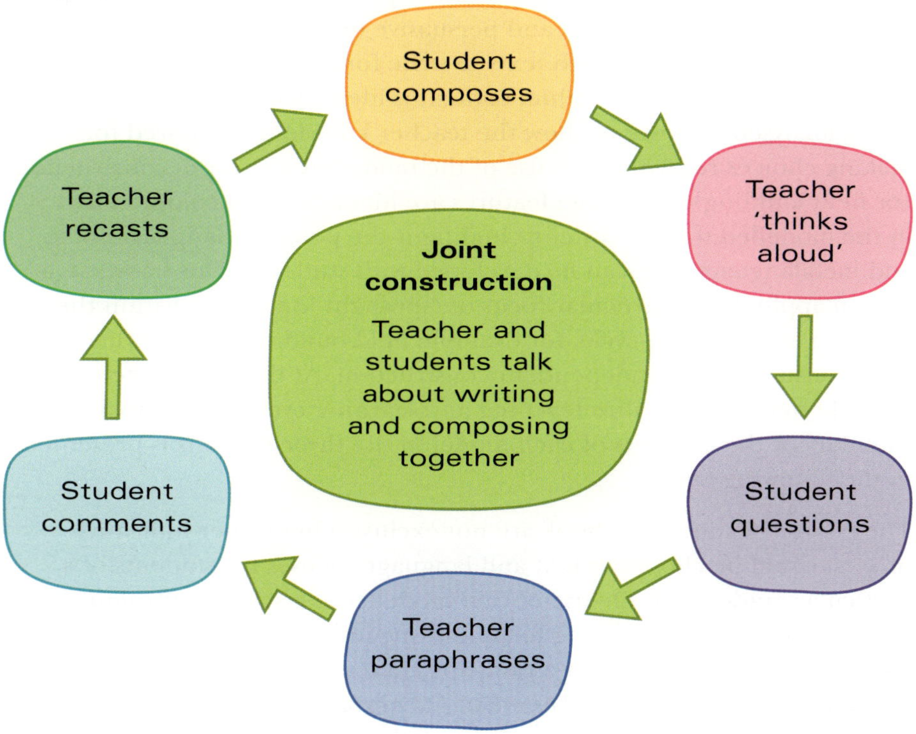

Figure 6 Elements for supporting students in joint construction (Rossbridge & Rushton, 2014)

Independent construction

At the point of independent construction, students can approach the development of a text similar to the one that has been modelled and/or jointly constructed. This may be on their own or with a partner, as they would have at this stage, talked their way into writing (Lemke, 1989). Individual students will have been able to problem solve with peers and the teacher, as mentor, would have answered questions about the subject matter and all the choices they will need to make when writing. Like all other aspects of the teaching and learning cycle the focus for independent writing is not solely on the production of a text as an objective but on supporting students to describe and defend their choices in developing a text.

How to use this book

The purpose of this introduction is to outline the process for developing knowledge about texts and language and then the application of such knowledge in supporting students through careful pedagogical choices. The three sections of the book that follow provide models for working with imaginative, informative and persuasive texts. In each section the models focus on working with texts to write for a particular purpose. Within each model a curriculum context is identified and then a modelled text is analysed in order to show the teacher knowledge required for making choices regarding the use of the modelled text for deconstruction (or field building). Language features are identified and colour coded in the modelled texts in order to highlight the potential language focus and metalanguage that can be developed with students. This knowledge is then applied to a particular focus or 'spotlight' on a stage within the teaching and learning cycle, for example field building, deconstruction, joint construction or independent construction. At the end of each model possible steps in the entire teaching and learning cycle are summarised. A summary of the contents of each model in the three sections is presented in the following table.

The choices made in this book are not exclusive but rather indicative of what could be chosen as text and language focuses for students of a particular grade. With the use of rich modelled texts and purposeful writing contexts, the teaching focus and suggestions presented in each model can be adapted across a range of grades. We have used the framework provided by the *Australian Curriculum: English*, looked at language, literature and literacy and noted the ways in which they overlap and inform each other across subject areas and grades.

Appendix 1 provides a table which tracks the development of grammatical knowledge across all the models. This is based on the *Australian Curriculum: English*. Appendix 2 provides a planning proforma which follows the process used for planning to 'put it in writing' throughout this book.

Section one			
Writing in the imaginative world			
Subject	English	English	English
Writing	Narrative	Literary recount	Narrative
Reading	*Don't let the pigeon drive the bus!*	*Silver Buttons*	*Blueback*
Language for expressing and connecting ideas		Verb groups (processes) and adverbial/ prepositional phrases (circumstances)	
Language for interacting with others	Speech functions: statement, question, offer, command Visual features: speech bubbles, demands, gestures, stance	Visual features: mid/long shots	Figurative language such as simile, metaphor and personification
Language for text structure and organisation			
Spotlight on the teaching and learning cycle	Independent writing	Text deconstruction	Text deconstruction

Section two			
Writing in the informative world			
Subject	Science	Geography	History
Writing	Procedural recount/ experiment report	Comparative report	Historical recount
Reading	*Race some beads*	*The difference between the Amazon and Daintree rainforests*	*Aliens*
Language for expressing and connecting ideas	Action, perceiving and relating verbs/processes, general and specific nouns/ participants, adverbials/ circumstances		Noun groups/ participants
Language for interacting with others			Vocabulary to convey perspective
Language for text structure and organisation		Word associations and conjunctions	
Spotlight on the teaching and learning cycle	Building the field	Joint construction (editing)	Independent writing

Section three			
Writing in the persuasive world			
Subject	English	Science	History
Writing	Discussion	Exposition	Exposition
Reading	*Parachute*	*School drop-off and pick-up zones*	'Stolen Child: Mathinna's story'
Language for expressing and connecting ideas		Connecting clauses and conjunctions	
Language for interacting with others	Evaluative vocabulary		
Language for text structure and organisation		Connectives	Nominalisation and passive voice
Spotlight on the teaching and learning cycle	Building the field	Text deconstruction	Independent writing

section one

Writing in the imaginative world

The writing of imaginative texts can take place in many subjects but occurs primarily in the English subject area. The *Australian Curriculum: English* (2012) states that the primary purpose of imaginative texts is to 'entertain through their imaginative use of literary elements. They are recognised for their form, style and artistic or aesthetic value'.

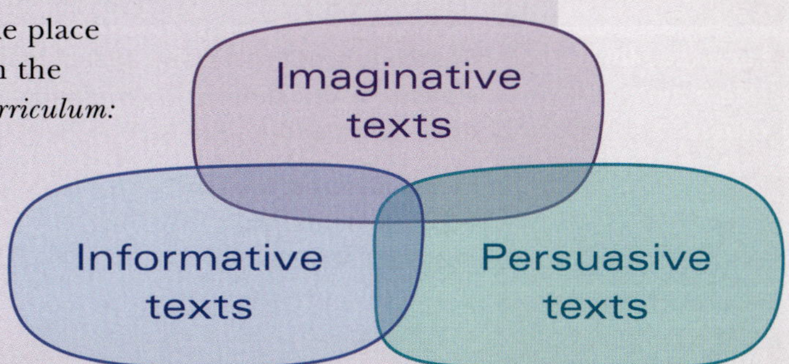

In this section, models of how to plan for and teach imaginative writing are included. They are:

- Model 1 Writing to interact with an audience (page 17)
- Model 2 Writing to recount imaginatively (page 31)
- Model 3 Writing to evoke feelings (page 44)

To support writing we have chosen modelled texts which we hope students will enjoy. They will also provide examples of language, structure and subject matter which will in turn will help students respond imaginatively by composing their own texts. When using literature as models, 'texts are chosen because they are judged to have potential for enriching the lives of students, expanding the scope of their experience, and because they represent effective and interesting features of form and style'. (ACARA, 2012). Well-written stories provide the reader with ideas and knowledge about the world and also the world of the imagination. Reading quality children's literature provides the reader with what Saxby calls 'hard knowledge' (Saxby, 1993, p. 58); ideas which can be used to create as well as comprehend text. In the table below the subject area, genre and language focus as well as the title of a text used for modelling/deconstruction provide an overview of the models in this section.

Writing in the imaginative world			
Subject	English	English	English
Writing	Narrative	Literary recount	Narrative
Reading	*Don't let the pigeon drive the bus!*	*Silver Buttons*	*Blueback*
Language for expressing and developing ideas		Verb groups (processes) and adverbial/prepositional phrases (circumstances)	
Language for interacting with others	Speech functions: statement, question, offer, command Visual features: speech bubbles, demands, gestures, stance	Visual features: mid/long shots	Figurative language such as simile, metaphor and personification
Language for text structure and organisation			
Spotlight on the teaching and learning cycle	Independent writing	Text deconstruction	Text deconstruction

model one

Writing to engage with an audience

Writing	Narrative
Reading	*Don't let the pigeon drive the bus!*
Language	Language for interacting with others – speech functions: statement, question, offer, command; visual features: speech bubbles, demands, gestures, stance
Supporting the student	Independent writing

The following teaching and learning sequence was developed in the English subject area and focuses on the role of multimodal texts in developing character through both verbal and visual choices. *Don't let the pigeon drive the bus!* (2004) is the first of a series of Pigeon books by Mo Willems. The characters interact directly with the audience as the bus driver asks the reader to watch his bus making sure the pigeon doesn't try to drive it. The pigeon draws on all his persuasive techniques to try to convince the reader to let him drive the bus.

Other Pigeon books by Mo Willems that draw on similar features include:

Don't let the pigeon stay up late!
The pigeon finds a hot dog!
The pigeon needs a bath!
The pigeon wants a puppy!

The app, *Don't Let the Pigeon Run this App!* (Disney, 2011) is an interactive version of the Pigeon books. It is useful for exploring Mo Willems' techniques. It also has a lesson on how to draw the pigeon and gives users the opportunities for creating other pigeon stories.

Knowledge about texts and language

The choice of the book *Don't let the pigeon drive the bus!* (Willems, 2004) is based on a close analysis of its features. The analysis that follows in Table 1 reveals the possibilities for investigating how interpersonal relationships can be developed through visual and verbal choices to shape an audience's reaction to a character.

Table 1 Analysis of features of *Don't let the pigeon drive the bus!*

Context	Mo Willems is a writer, animator and multi-award winning children's book author. His series of highly engaging, humorous, imaginative picture books featuring the opinionated pigeon were created out of books that he had written for his own children as well as the influence of 'interesting characters' growing up in New Orleans (Hyperion Books for Children, 2008). The books integrate text and image to create a coherent unit whilst they also operate beyond just the context of the picture book, as the character of the pigeon has been further developed through additional texts including websites, tweets, an app and videos. Technology has given the pigeon a life beyond the book.
Social purpose/ genre	*Don't let the pigeon drive the bus!* is an imaginative text in that its social purpose is to entertain through a non-traditional story or anecdote (Martin & Rose, 2008). The text also contains persuasive elements as the characters come alive through a range of interpersonal devices. The purpose is achieved through a strong focus on character development and interaction with the reader across the stages of the text.
Field (What is the subject matter?)	*Don't let the pigeon drive the bus!* contains two characters or participants, the pigeon and the bus driver. The pigeon dominates the action across the text by engaging with the reader throughout in seeking permission to drive the bus and by communicating primarily through speech bubbles. Action processes are mainly communicated through the visuals. The setting isn't important to the text as the emphasis is on engaging with the main character.
Tenor (Who is involved and what is the relationship?)	Mo Willems makes a deliberate choice in the book to interact with the audience through the characters. Through combinations of visual and verbal choices the reader is not only invited into the text but also experiences the developing attitude of the pigeon. This makes for a highly engaging, humorous text to read aloud as demonstrated by Mo Willems in numerous video clips (Hyperion Books for Children, 2008). The power of the interpersonal features is summed up by Mo Willems himself, when he states that he only 'creates 51% of the book' (Wish TV, YouTube, 2014) as the rest of the interaction comes from the reader. The pigeon elicits a response from the reader through the unity of visual/verbal resources making it almost impossible for the reader not to respond to him.

Mode (What is the channel of communication?)	*Don't let the pigeon drive the bus!* is a multimodal text as the combination of words and images creates a coherent whole. It is an unusual example of a narrative form in that language is being used to provoke the reader and character in the book to interact with each other as opposed to more traditional narratives where language is used as reflection.
Text structure and phases	The narrative structure of orientation, complication and resolution (Martin & Rose, 2008), which is inserted before the text opens, is organised with the bus driver only appearing in a minimal orientation to ask the reader not to let the pigeon drive the bus and at the end to thank the reader for not letting the pigeon drive the bus. The complication is that the pigeon wants to drive the bus even though he is not really equipped to do so. Throughout, the events lead to the escalation of the pigeon's emotions where he loses his patience with the reader. The pigeon varies the way he addresses the reader in order to structure the development of his character across the text. The phases, which are flexible choices made within the stages of the text, reveal intricate choices made by Mo Willems around the combination of events, interactions and reactions. The events in particular (see Table 2) are structured by choices regarding speech functions in speech bubbles combined with other visual features. These events are structured through interactions and reactions by the pigeon. It is only in the beginning and end of the text that the pigeon communicates with visuals in thought bubbles as he aspires to drive a bus and then a truck.

Understanding features of a modelled text

Through analysis of *Don't let the pigeon drive the bus!* the text and language features that have been identified assist in determining a focus for developing a teaching sequence. In this analysis the following colour coding has been used to identify the speech functions (see Table 2).

statement   question   command   offer

Table 2 Text structure, phases and language features analysis

Text structure	Phases	Extract from *Don't let the pigeon drive the bus!* (Willems, 2004)
Sequence of events	Request Reaction	Hey, can I drive the bus? Please? I'll be careful. I know what, I'll just steer.

		My cousin Harry drives a bus almost every day!
		True story.
		VROOM-VROOM VROOMY VROOM-VROOM!
		PIGEON AT THE WHEEL!
		No?
		I never get to do anything!
	Suggestion	Hey, I've got an idea. Let's play 'Drive the Bus'!
		I'll go first!
		C'mon! Just to the corner and back!
		I'll be your best friend!
		How 'bout I give you a fiver?
	Reaction	No fair!
		I bet your mum would let me.
		What's the problem!?
		It's just a bus!!!
		I have dreams you know!
		Fine.
		LET ME DRIVE THE BUS!!!

Focus on language (and image) for interacting with others

The tenor of a text relates to the interpersonal aspects at play as an author interacts with an audience. In *Don't let the pigeon drive the bus!* the patterns of interaction reflect the relationship between the pigeon and the audience.

Through the pigeon, Mo Willems draws on combinations of speech functions through careful clause choices to interact with the audience and express attitude (see Derewianka, 2011) as seen in the colour coded speech functions in Table 2.

- statements (provide information)
- questions (ask for information)
- commands (ask someone to do something or give something)
- offers (offer to do or provide something)

These choices are integrated into the visual through the use of speech bubbles. Of note is the increased use of exclamation marks as a visual/verbal feature as the text progresses, and the pigeon's response increases in intensity.

Both the bus driver and pigeon stimulate the interaction initially through the use of questions to engage the reader by eliciting a response from the reader (NO!). Throughout the events, the pigeon relies mainly on the use of statements with interspersed questions (see Figure 1). Then we see a sequence of offers (see Figure 2) as he takes on new tactics of persuasion. It is not until the crescendo where the pigeon yells 'LET ME DRIVE THE BUS!!!' that we note the use of a command (See Figure 3). It is at this point where the extreme emotion of the pigeon character reacting to the audience becomes a consequence of prior interactions through the book. The audience becomes partly responsible for his reaction, which adds to the humour. Visually we see the appearance of multiple pigeons, referred to as 'upscaling', (Painter, Martin and Unsworth, 2013, p. 45) across a double page spread all of which emphasise his reaction (see Figure 3).

Based on the minimalist drawing style with limited detail and depth, (Painter, Martin & Unsworth, 2013) it could be said that the pigeon lacks credibility or a connection with reality, which adds to the fun and the ridiculousness of the idea of a pigeon driving a bus. The particular style of drawing with circles and ovals as the basic shapes, small circles for the eyes, restriction to side head angles, oversized facial features and the openness of the beak guides the reader to create inferences about his feelings. This combines with the pigeon's gestures ranging from pleading and whispering to waving and arm crossing. Choices show his stance, often at a frontal angle more so at the beginning of the book, creating greater involvement due to increased use of oblique angles later in the book resulting in less intimacy with the audience as he becomes more despondent (Callow, 2013).

A social relationship between pigeon and reader is further established with the gaze of the pigeon as he frequently makes demands by looking straight at the reader. The pigeon's attitude expressed visually in combination with his actual speech creates the interaction.

Figure 1 Figures 1, 2 and 3 – deconstructing the text by annotating features

Figure 2

The colour choices also complement the mood of the character creating an interpersonal look and feel. The choice of a muted background colour also results in a removal from reality (Painter, Martin & Unsworth, 2013) as does the removal of setting which places greater emphasis on the emotions and behaviour of the pigeon further evoking affect and judgement. In addition to colour, choice of font (Figure 3) can also suggest an action or in this case emotion (Callow, 2013).

By considering the unity of the images of the pigeon and the speech bubbles, there are many possibilities for the analysis of the interrelation of the verbal and visual features. It also shows how the interpersonal features unify the reader into the experience, resulting in the reader's feelings ranging from affection and warmth to sheer annoyance towards the main character.

The sticky notes on Figures 1, 2 and 3 offer guidelines on deconstructing the features of this text. They can be viewed as annotations of the various features of the text. Placing the sticky notes on the text is a useful device to record observations and analyse both text and image.

Figure 3

The *Australian Curriculum: English* in Year 1 identifies the following content.

Language	Understand that language is used in combination with other means of communication, for example facial expressions and gestures to interact with others (ACELA1444)
	Understand that there are different ways of asking for information, making offers and giving commands (ACELA1446)
	Explore different ways of expressing emotions, including verbal, visual, body language and facial expressions (ACELA1787)
	Recognise that different types of punctuation, including full stops, question marks and exclamation marks, signal sentences that make statements, ask questions, express emotion or give commands (ACELA1449)
Literature	Discuss how authors create characters using language and images (ACELT1581)
	Recreate texts imaginatively using drawing, writing, performance and digital forms of communication (ACELT1586)
Literacy	Construct texts that incorporate supporting images using software including word processing programs (ACELY1664)

This content can be addressed based on teacher preparation and knowledge about *Don't let the pigeon drive the bus!* and its features, as is suggested in the next section.

Supporting the learner

The following teaching and learning sequence (Figure 4) is based on the teacher's knowledge of verbal and visual features of *Don't let the pigeon drive the bus!* It outlines steps to support students in integrating features to convey character through direct interaction with an audience. In the example below the focus is on independent construction as an exemplar of one stage within the teaching and learning cycle.

Figure 4
Adapted teaching and learning cycle

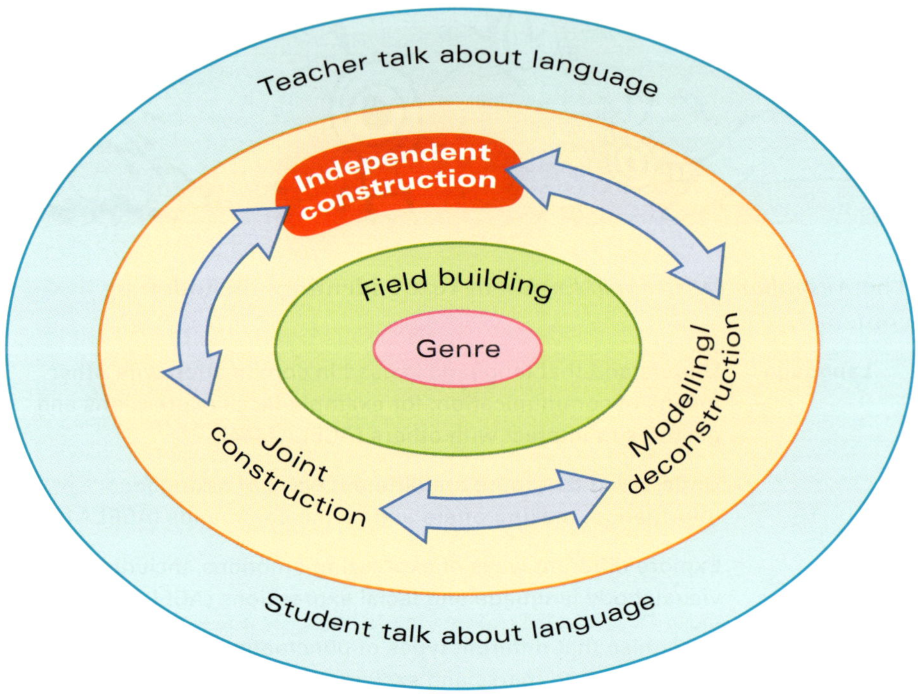

Spotlight on language for interacting with others during independent writing

This detailed example of independent construction focuses on composing multimodal text by drawing upon language developed throughout the teaching sequence. Through identifying the combination of written and visual features in the modelled text and during joint construction, students are equipped to make choices in composing their own texts.

Plan for writing by revising the techniques used by Mo Willems in enabling his character to engage with the audience and communicate his feelings, as shown in Figure 5. Making metalanguage explicit throughout the teaching sequence assists students in making informed choices and provides opportunities to discuss and reflect on choices (Rossbridge & Rushton, 2010).

Figure 5 Visual and verbal features

VISUAL

Feature	Purpose
demands	to make eye contact with the audience
position and size of the pupil	to show the character's feelings
open beak/mouth	to show the character is speaking
facing front on	to make a close connection to the audience
facing side on	to be more distant from the audience
action lines or moving body parts (vectors)	to show actions
repeated images of the character	to show escalation of feelings
speech bubbles	to show what the character says to the audience
thought bubbles	to show the audience what the character is thinking
exclamation marks	to emphasise feelings
statements	to give information to persuade the audience
questions	to get a response from the audience
offers	to offer to do something to persuade further
commands	to tell the audience to do something

VERBAL

Ask the class to think of their own character in order to complete a new title 'Don't let the _____ ______ the _____!' Remind students that we want to compose a text or story like Mo Willems' story, so our choice of character needs to be funny and perhaps a little ridiculous. In the following example (Figure 6), the students chose 'Don't let the puppy ride the bike!'

With a partner one student 'sculpts' another as they physically negotiate the representation of their character by showing body language, stance and gestures at the beginning, middle and end of the events in their story. Sculpting supports students to demonstrate understanding of the visual features through their own non-verbal communication skills. It also provides the opportunity for thinking more deeply about the character (Hertzberg, 2012).

Allocate the beginning, middle or end of the text to pairs of students in the class so that they draw their character with an empty speech bubble. Working in pairs and practising in different modes allows students to rehearse and develop ideas and language choices and is integral to planning for composing a text and for moving from speaking to writing. Add students' images to the ChatterPix app (Figure 6), which allows students to record voices with their images. Students record what the pigeon might say whilst considering the stage of the text. Once students are happy that their choice reflects what the pigeon is communicating in

Figure 6 Recording using the ChatterPix app

Figure 7 Independent construction of phases in the example text 'Don't let the puppy ride the bike!'

the image they add the question, statement, offer or command into the drawn speech bubble. By considering how the visual and written text work together, the multimodal nature of the text is acknowledged as all the features combine to create meaning (Callow, 2013; Painter, Martin & Unsworth, 2013).

Place all images together and as a class sequence them based on how the character communicates with the audience and conveys feelings. Remind students of the list of techniques used by Mo Willems and the order in which they were used throughout his book. Encourage students to talk about their choices by referring to features. Remember that making metalanguage explicit throughout the teaching sequence assists students in making informed choices and provides opportunities to discuss and reflect on choices (Rossbridge & Rushton, 2010).

Summary of a teaching and learning sequence

Building the field

- Show images of pigeons and brainstorm their typical behaviours.
- Locate texts that contain pigeons and discuss whether they are most likely to be found in imaginative or informative texts.

Text deconstruction/modelled reading

- Show the cover of *Don't let the pigeon drive the bus!* Predict the type of text, the target audience and what the character of the pigeon might be like. Plot predictions about the pigeon on the diagram (Figure 8) and return to the predictions after reading.
- Read the book, encouraging students to respond to the pigeon.
- After reading return to predictions (Figure 8) and discuss how Mo Willems engaged the audience and created feelings about the pigeon. Develop a list of features and add to it throughout the reading referring to the model in Figure 5.

Figure 8
Predicting the pigeon's actions

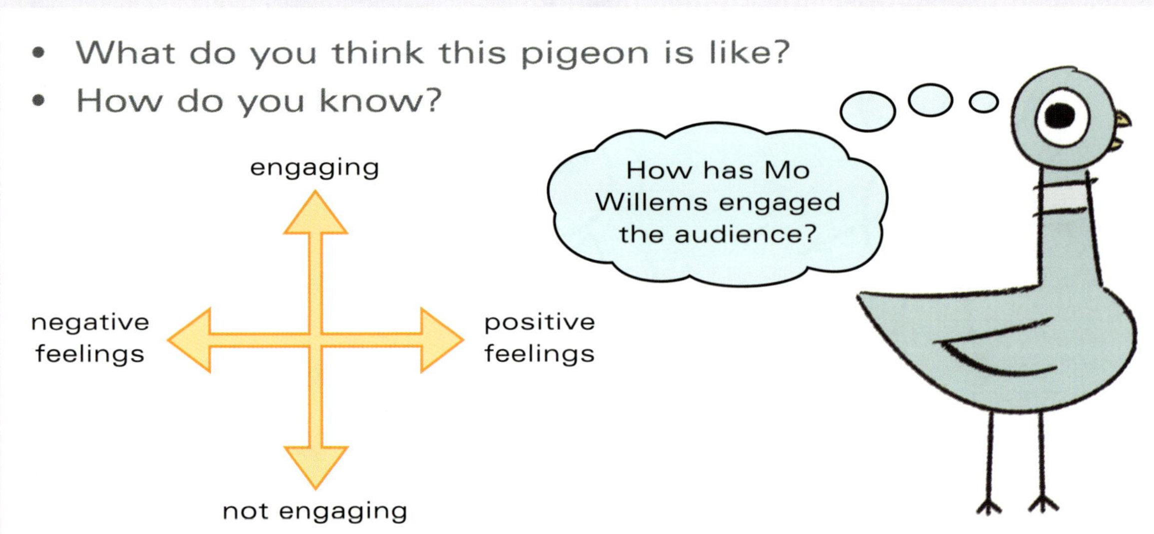

- Using the 'Don't Let the Pigeon Run this App' (Disney Publishing Worldwide Applications, 2011) watch the lesson on how to draw the pigeon.
- Select images of the pigeon from across the text and annotate the features, eg, speech bubbles, head, beak and eye position and shape, gestures and stance (see Figures 1–3).
- Identify types of speech functions the pigeon uses throughout the text, i.e. questions, statements, offers and commands and link to text structure/phases and character development.
- Use the sculpting drama strategy, (Hertzberg, 2012), where students 'sculpt' their partner to show how the pigeon might look and feel at the beginning, middle and end of the events.

Joint construction

- Tell students that they are going to develop a different character to the pigeon but use Mo Willem's techniques for engaging with the audience and conveying emotion.
- Divide a whiteboard into three and draw the new character at three different points across the happenings in the story by discussing features. Share the pen with students. Ensure the choices made in the image support the written choice in the speech bubble by practising again through sculpting. Discuss potential audience reaction.

Independent construction

- Revise visual and verbal techniques used by Mo Willems.
- Develop a new character.
- Repeat sculpting for the new character.
- Pairs develop multimodal text for the beginning, middle or end of the text using ChatterPix app.
- Develop text on paper and sequence all pages as a a whole class, discussing choices.

Resources

Disney Publishing Worldwide Applications 2011, 'Don't let the pigeon run this app!' mobile app, viewed 7 April 2015, < https://itunes.apple.com/au/app/dont-let-pigeon-run-this-app!/id459749670?mt=8 >.

Duck Duck Mouse Inc, 2013 'ChatterPix Kids mobile app', viewed 7 April 2015, < https://itunes.apple.com/au/app/chatterpix-kids-by-duck-duck/id734046126?mt=8 >.

Hyperion Books for Children 2008, 'Mo History', viewed 7 April 2015, <http://www.pigeonpresents.com/grownup.aspx >.

NBC Learn 2012, 'Writers speak to kids: Mo Willems', viewed 7 April 2015, <https://www.nbclearn.com/writersspeak/cuecard/60820>.

Willems, M 2004, *Don't let the pigeon drive the bus!* Walker Books, London.

Willems, M 2005, *The pigeon finds a hot dog!* Walker Books, London.

Willems, M 2007, *Don't let the pigeon stay up late!* Walker Books, London.

Willems, M 2008 *The pigeon wants a puppy!* Walker Books, London.

Willems, M 2014, *The pigeon needs a bath!* Walker Books, London.

Wish TV 2014, Mo Willems, Author, viewed 7 April 2015, <https://www.youtube.com/watch?v=UVCdI-yALZc >.

model two

Writing to recount imaginatively

Writing	Imaginative recount
Reading	*Silver Buttons*
Language	Language for expressing ideas: verb groups (processes) and adverbial/ prepositional phrases (circumstances); visual features: mid/long shots
Supporting the student	Text deconstruction

This teaching and learning sequence was developed in the English subject area with the aim of students crafting their own written texts as a result of engagement with, and appreciation of literature, particularly picture books. The picture book *Silver Buttons* by Bob Graham (2013) can be categorised as a type of story genre as it focuses on a range of events in the world of imagination. It serves as an effective model for recounting a small slice of time. A moment in time is captured as 'the book is studded with little cameos of both everyday events and momentous occasions, all part of the rich tapestry of human life' (Stephenson, 2014). It is very carefully crafted and aesthetically pleasing. Being simple and at the same time complex enough, it can be used with a range of students for multiple purposes to focus on multimodal features.

Figure 1
Mid shot from
Silver Buttons

Knowledge about texts and language

Silver Buttons has been chosen based on a close analysis of its features. Students can engage with the book for enjoyment, while at the same time its features lend themselves to an appreciation of literary themes and literacy development as shown in Table 1.

Table 1 Analysis of features of *Silver Buttons*

Context	Published in 2013, *Silver Buttons* represents, and has evolved out of, a contemporary urban Western community context in which individuals are involved in simple, everyday events as well as more significant life events. It can be interpreted as a comment on the busyness of contemporary society and the attention paid to key or more mundane moments in time.
Social purpose/ genre	The social purpose of the book is to entertain whilst also considering culturally held values and beliefs (Christie & Derewianka, 2008). The text has narrative elements but as it is written as a brief snapshot of time it does not involve the typical complication found in traditional narratives thus reflecting aspects of the literary or imaginative recount genre. 'There are many different types of stories. Not all of them involve a Complication' (Derewianka & Jones, 2012, p. 64).
Field (What is the subject matter?)	The events of the book take place for the duration of one minute. Jonathan is Jodie's little brother and in that minute, as Jodie draws the last silver button on her duck's boot, Jonathan achieves the important 'milestone' of taking his first steps (Figure 1). This event coincides with a range of other events occurring simultaneously across the city.
Tenor (Who is involved and what is the relationship?)	Bob Graham takes the role of narrator who along with the reader is positioned as an onlooker of the events. The shared 'everydayness' of the events in conjunction with the momentous first steps of Jonathan, the farewell of a soldier and the birth of a baby create the tenor. The theme of the celebration of 'everyday' events conveys the interpersonal relationship. The images use mid shots that create a closer relationship between the character of Jonathan and the audience. As opposed to this, longer shots are used to convey contextual information about other participants and events across the city (Figure 2).
Mode (What is the channel of communication?)	Although the written language may appear simplistic and is supported by the visual choices in showing actions of participants and movement of circumstances from the home to the broader city, the choices are very carefully constructed with choices at clause level organising the whole text.

Text structure and phases	As the social purpose and literary recount genre determine the overall structure of the text, we can see that the author has drawn on the typical recount text structure of orientation, series of events and reorientation. However, this structure is slightly complex and unpredictable moving from the generic recounts and narratives often constructed by students. The text begins with a predictable orientation introducing characters in a setting of time. This is then unusually disrupted by the title page of the text. This disruption or pausing of the orientation cleverly places time on hold along with Jodie's pen as the reader gradually realises all events are occurring during the same minute. This affects the events through the middle of the text as the focus is not so much on temporal ordering of events but on simultaneous occurrences. The images also structure the text as the orientation and reorientation are depicted within the living room of the family with mid shots of Jonathan but the record of events take place in ever expanding places across the community. By digging more deeply into the text we can see the use of phases which in this case are quite repetitive particularly in the record of events resulting in the representation of simultaneous events. The one use of dialogue at the end of the text draws attention to the significant event that has occurred. (See Table 2)

Figure 2 Long shot from *Silver Buttons*

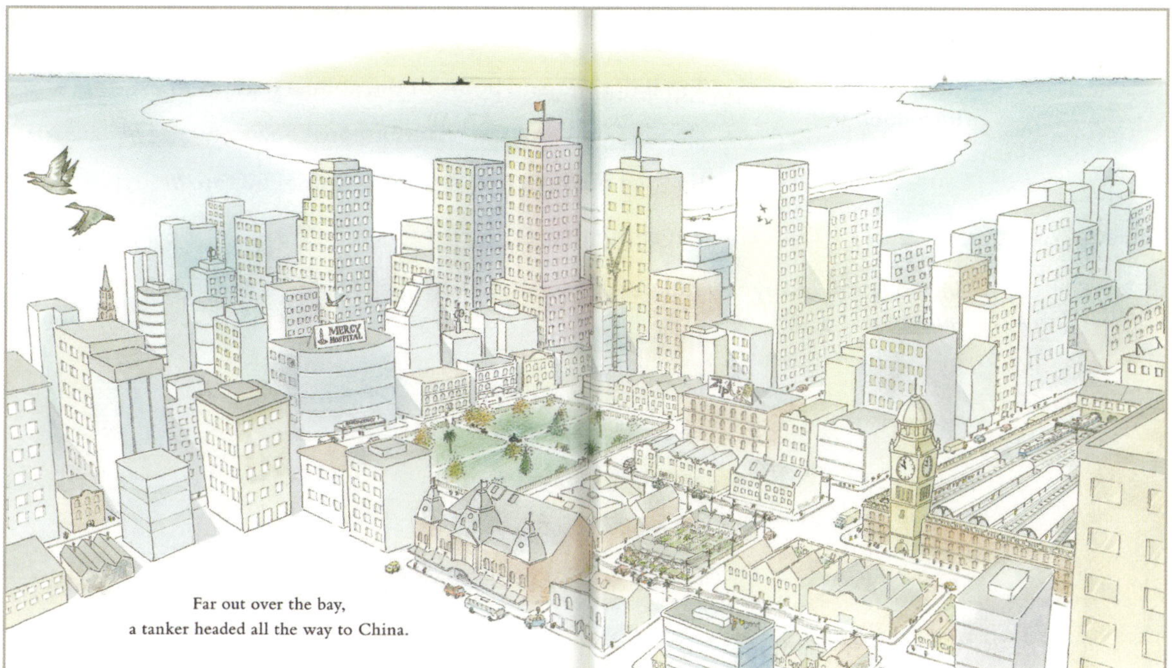

Understanding features of a modelled text

In the analysis of *Silver Buttons* in Table 2, text and language features have been identified which assist in determining a focus for developing a teaching sequence. The following colour coding has been used to analyse the text:

noun groups/participants
verb groups/processes
adverbials/circumstances

The following symbols signal:

end of a clause //
end of a clause at the end of a sentence ///

Table 2 Analysis of text and language features

Text structure	Phases	Excerpts from *Silver Buttons* by Bob Graham
Orientation	Introduction of setting of time	At 9.59 on Thursday morning, Jodie drew a duck. ///
	Character introduction	Top hat, cane and boots of the softest leather. /// On the boots she put silver buttons: one ... two ... /// Her pen hovered in the air for the final button. ///
Title		*Silver Buttons*
	Introduction of key event	Jodie's brother Jonathan pushed slowly to his feet. /// He swayed, // he frowned, // he tilted forward ... // and took his first step. /// He took that step // like he was going somewhere. ///

Record of events	Movement to multiple events across setting of place	At that moment, Jonathan's mum played "Merrily Kiss the Quaker's Wife" on her tin whistle. /// Mum loved the picture of the wild hare on her calendar so much, // she hadn't changed it in three years. /// Outside, a pigeon nested under the roof. /// As Jonathan took his first step, // a feather floated gently past the window like an autumn leaf. /// Next door, Alice posted sticks through the front gate ... // and an early-morning jogger puffed on by. /// Out in the street, Joseph Pascano avoided the cracks in the path // so the sharks wouldn't get him. /// ... Far out over the bay, a tanker headed all the way to China. ///
Reorientation	Return to initial setting and characters	Then down came Jonathan on his little pink knees. ///
	Dialogue to emphasise main event	"Mummy!" yelled Jodie. /// "Jonathan's just taken his first step". /// Jodie put the last silver button on her duck's boots. ///
	Reorientating setting of time and place	Sunlight from all over the city streamed through the window // and the kitchen clock struck ten. ///

Focus on language for expressing ideas

The field is built through the choices of participants, processes and circumstances within the clauses throughout the text. The groups within clauses in *Silver Buttons* represents what is going on in the world (See Derewianka, 2011; Humphrey, Droga & Feez, 2012). As the clause is the basic unit of meaning for expressing ideas we can ask the following questions:

- Who or what is taking part? (participants)
- What is going on? (processes)
- What circumstances surround the activity? (circumstances eg, when, where, how)

By asking these questions our attention is drawn to the chunks of meaning in the text. These alert us to the patterns in the text, which in turn make us reflect on how the author achieves the purpose through the genre. In *Silver Buttons* the participants are represented through noun groups, the processes are verb groups and the circumstances tend to be adverbial/prepositional phrases. The participants reflect the text structure as Jonathan and Jodie are present in the orientation and reorientation stages. The other participants appear through many events, most of which involve action processes. Of note is the position of adverbial/prepositional phrases at the beginning of clauses, in Theme position (Derewianka, 2011) within the record of events. This structures the text, taking the reader on the journey and emphasises the shifts in place settings.

The *Australian Curriculum: English* in Year 4 identifies the following content which can be addressed based on teacher preparation and knowledge about texts and language.

Language	Understand that the meaning of sentences can be enriched through the use of noun groups/phrases and verb groups/phrases and prepositional phrases (ACELA1493)
	Understand how adverb groups/phrases and prepositional phrases work in different ways to provide circumstantial details about an activity (ACELA1495)
Literature	Use metalanguage to describe the effects of ideas, text structures and language features of literary texts (ACELT1604)
	Create literary texts that explore students' own experiences and imagining (ACELT1607)
Literacy	Identify characteristic features used in imaginative, informative and persuasive texts to meet the purpose of the text (ACELY1690)
	Use comprehension strategies to build literal and inferred meaning to expand content knowledge, integrating and linking ideas and analysing and evaluating texts (ACELY1692)

Supporting the learner

Based on teacher knowledge about text and language, the following teaching and learning sequence outlines steps to support students in moving from responding to text to composing text about events representing momentous occasions. It has a spotlight upon text deconstruction (see Figure 3). The focus is not only on the language features but also the theme of celebrating the ordinary events of life.

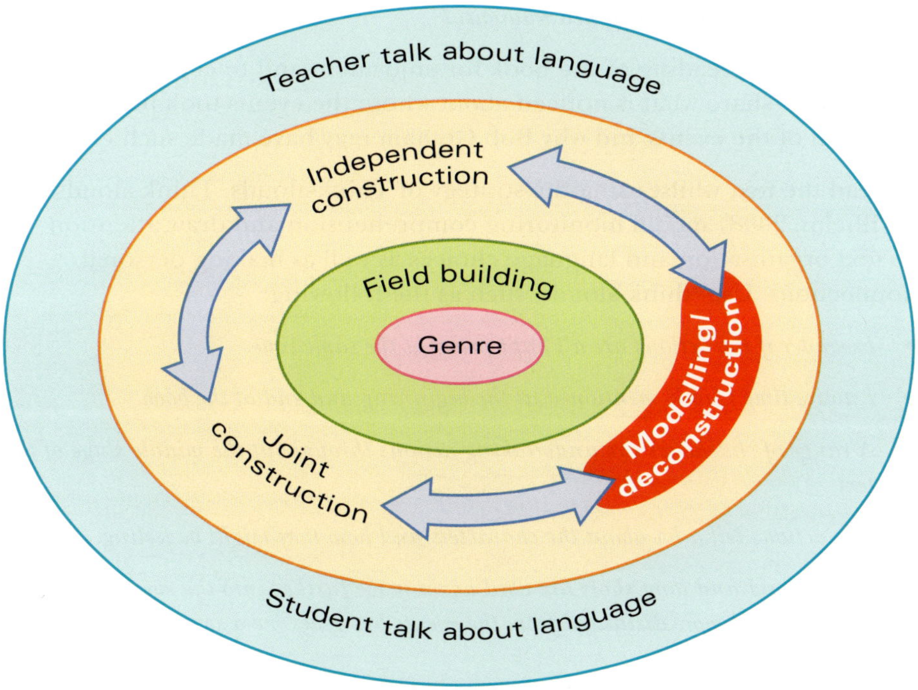

Figure 3
Adapted teaching and learning cycle with emphasis on deconstruction

Spotlight on language for expressing ideas during text deconstruction through modelled reading

This detailed example shows how to engage with meaning making and the language choices made by Bob Graham in *Silver Buttons,* using text deconstruction as the focus for modelling. It can be drawn upon when composing similar texts.

Show the front and back covers of *Silver Buttons* and ask students to predict content of the book, with questions such as:

- *Will the text be imaginative, informative or persuasive?*
- *What will the purpose be?*
- *What actions might occur and who might the actors be?*
- *Where might the events take place?*
- *What period of time might be covered across the text?*
- *Who is the author's imagined audience?*

After an initial reading of the book for enjoyment and to confirm predictions share what is noticed about where the events took place, the duration of the events and why Bob Graham may have made such choices.

Reread the text whilst using the strategy of Think-alouds. Think-alouds (Wilhelm, 2008) model monitoring comprehension and draw attention to text organisation and language choices as well as making personal connections. Use 'think-alouds' such as the following:

- *I wonder if the actions are all happening at the same time.*
- *I notice time is only mentioned at the beginning and end of the book.*
- *A range of characters are undertaking actions throughout the middle stage of the text.*
- *The actions tell a lot about the characters and how they might be feeling.*
- *I notice mid and long shots are used as we move further into the events. This makes me feel more distanced from the events but gives me a sense of the setting of the city.*
- *Some of these events remind me of milestones like learning how to ride a bike. I can remember when my daughters first learnt to walk. That was a milestone.*

Once students are familiar with the text, share or jointly develop criteria for composing similar texts (see Figure 4). Criteria communicate expectations and make learning visible while framing feedback during the lesson sequence (Hattie, 2012). Explicit criteria contain metalanguage (Schleppegrell, 2013) reflecting knowledge about the text and the choices made by the writer. This later assists students to make similar choices and reflect upon them in their own writing.

Criteria for writing

- the first event is a milestone
- verbs/processes cause the reader to infer character feelings
- use of adverbial/ prepositional phrases show movement of events across places
- images of setting show mid shots and long shots which structure the text

Figure 4
Criteria for writing

With further close reading of the initial pages of the text, the words used for Jonathan's actions can be highlighted (*pushed, swayed, frowned, tilted*). These words can be described as action verbs showing what is going on or the processes but that they also give hints about the character. In another colour the text can be annotated with words, which help us to infer Jonathan's character (*determined, unsure, worried*). The written and visual choices indicating actions convey that this is a milestone in Jonathan's life.

Figure 5
Making inferences about character by focusing on the choice of action verb

In groups students can repeat the process by annotating other pages of text (see Figure 5). Group work when analysing pages from the text serves as handover (Dufficy, 2005) from the modelling by the teacher. Students also have the support of other students and opportunities to respond with talk about the text.

During additional readings further attention can be drawn to text organisation and language choices involving aspects of time and place. For example: When it says, 'At that moment', Jonathan's mum is busy when he takes his first step. This leads to other events taking place to other people who are not aware of Jonathan's achievement. We can ask why Bob Graham begins to take us outside the house and into the street by placing phrases about circumstances of place at the beginning of clauses. This, in combination with the images, takes the reader away from the house to the street, local community and then to the city and beyond. Written and visual features are discussed simultaneously to show how they are working together (Callow, 2013).

During modelled identification of the adverbial phrases of place, discuss how they are adding information to the verbs/actions about where the action is occurring (circumstances of place). The phrases can be placed on a diagram to show moving from the home to the street to the city etc. This diagram (Figure 6) can be used later to support students planning their own writing.

Figure 6
Unpacking and planning diagram

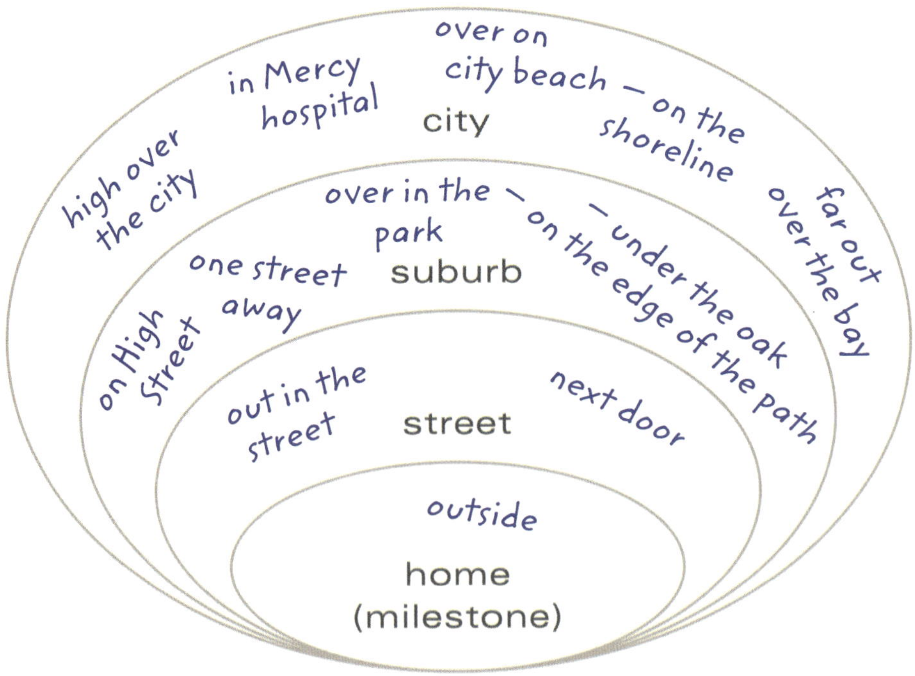

Deconstructing *Silver Buttons* through modelled reading, enables students to use the knowledge about language developed during reading, to develop their own text about a personal milestone. In the example of a student's writing (Figure 7), careful choices have been made with the verbs to ensure they cause the reader to make inferences about how the participant was feeling during the event. After writing, students annotate their own work and reflect on the writing criteria (see Figure 4). It is also important to continue the discussion about how language choices can enhance appreciation and enjoyment of texts and how the knowledge developed can be applied to other contexts and texts.

Figure 7
Independent writing

Obviously this text can be further developed to capitalise on the craft of Bob Graham by adding events which happen simultaneously in broader parts of the community with the placement of the circumstance of place at the beginning of each event. Photographs could be taken across the community with a focus on using mid and long shots to structure the text as events move further from the initial milestone.

Summary of a teaching and learning sequence

Building the field

- Identify daily activities, how they are shared and their significance.
- Sort images into everyday events and milestones.

Text deconstruction/modelled reading

- Make predictions and use 'think-alouds' to read the book.
- Develop criteria based on the writing technique used by Bob Graham.
- Identify action verbs/processes and make inferences about characters.
- Link the use of adverbial phrases/circumstances of time and place and visual features to structure of the text.

Joint construction

- Develop criteria for composing.
- Provide an image of a personal event /milestone as well as other images of events that may occur at the same time but in different places.
- Jointly plan by sequencing images and crop to move from mid to long shots.
- Annotate images with verbs providing inferences about character and adverbials moving from local to community settings.
- Jointly write text to accompany the images with discussion focused on verb choice and adverbials in first position of clauses during the events.

Independent construction

- Students bring a photo or draw a milestone. Students annotate an image with verbs and plan adverbials on a planning sheet. Students construct own text including images.
- Students peer and self-assess based on criteria.

Resources

Graham, B 2013, *Silver Buttons*, Walker Books, Sydney.

model three

Writing to evoke feelings

Writing	Narrative
Reading	*Blueback*
Language	Language for expressing ideas and interacting with others: figurative language such as simile, metaphor and personification
Supporting the student	Text deconstruction

Tim Winton, a much-awarded author, writes for both adults and children and while *Blueback* (Winton, 1997) is a story suitable for upper primary students of English, it will engage both children and adults. It has been reprinted several times and most recently released in hardback and in ebook format. The story is of a boy coming of age but it is his link with his home and family, which guides his development. His relationship with the fish *Blueback* symbolises his relationship with the environment in which he grew up and his desire to protect it is as understandable as the love one feels for a friend or family member.

Figure 1 Abel has a special relationship with Blueback the groper

Blueback is used here as a modelled text for looking at how Tim Winton uses figurative language to evoke feelings. Knowledge about this use of language is developed first through text deconstruction and then applied to joint and independent construction.

Knowledge about texts and language

There are many aspects of this story – its plot, themes and characters which will engage young readers but the telling of the story and the masterful use of language may also intrigue and invite young authors into the text. Close analysis of the text reveals that the author draws upon many tools for evoking feeling and emotion in the reader, as shown in Table 1.

Table 1 Analysis of features of *Blueback*

Context	Tim Winton's love of nature, particularly as a Western Australian, is demonstrated in his love of the sea and especially of the Ningaloo reef. His involvement in protecting that reef and others around Australia, and what he values in the natural environment is reflected in this story as much as in his speeches and articles relating to saving Ningaloo and all reefs (See: https://www.wilderness.org.au/articles/tim-wintons-ningaloo-reef-rally-speech). His activism is ongoing and related to the sea and to the protection of all marine life. (http://www.wwf.org.au/?4120/Author-Tim-Winton-on-his-love-for-the-sea-and-our-generations-opportunity-to-protect-it http://www.marineconservation.org.au/news.php/278/author-tim-winton-in-sydney-to-promote-marine-conservation)
Social purpose/ genre	Narratives entertain but authors also often take a stance on an issue and comment or reflect on the behaviour of individuals or groups in their societies. Stories engage when the viewer or reader can connect with the story. 'True literature nourishes the mind, promotes sensory awareness, develops emotional sensitivity and provides a rich linguistic environment. Well-written fiction, along with good non-fiction, nourishes the mind with facts, as well as with ideas – what could be called "hard knowledge".'(Saxby, 1993, p. 58)
Field (What is the subject matter?)	*Blueback* is an ideal novel for young people as the subject matter is both engaging and challenging. The novel deals with a current issue in our society, the protection of the natural environment, as well as with the age-old issues of family, relationships and growing up. The focal point in this novel is the relationship that the main character, Abel, has with a gigantic blue groper that he names Blueback (see Figure 1). The adventures Abel experiences growing up in Longboat Bay are adventures in nature and his relationship to nature will captivate young readers wherever they live.

Tenor (Who is involved and what is the relationship?)	For young readers, whether fluent or struggling, this novel presents the perfect opportunity to enjoy the work of an author who has a masterful command of the English language. The presentation is welcoming rather than daunting, providing a real bridge between illustrated stories and novels. To invite the reader into the text, the chapters are quite short, no more than ten or so pages and at the beginning of each chapter there is a black and white drawing of something from the sea: a shell, a seahorse, a crab. The language resources used to tell this story encompass all the rich figurative language that could be found in a narrative – simile, metaphor, alliteration and personification. These function to not only tell about the subject matter, but through the use of figurative language to engage the reader.
Mode (What is the channel of communication?)	The role of language in this text exemplifies the written mode as it is being used to develop a story as a product not as part of an interactive process. The channel of communication is graphic or written and the medium is written. The aspects of mode include the role of language which may be central or constitutive of the text as opposed to ancillary. The channel of communication could be for instance sound waves or writing – phonic or graphic. The medium also may be spoken or written and the text is either developed through a process of interaction or as a product. It is the combination of these factors which define the mode.

Understanding features of a modelled text

Examples of simile, metaphor and personification have been identified across this text in Table 2 and can be explicitly taught by examining how Tim Winton uses noun and verbal groups and prepositional phrases to develop these features.

In Table 2 the column on the left very briefly summarises the plot as it unfolds during the arc of the narrative. For students who are not fluent readers outlining the plot in this way can support reading. It frees the student to focus on the characterisation and the development of themes in the novel rather than focusing on 'What happened?'. This question, too often asked, does not help a reader to engage at a deeper level with the text. Rather the column on the right provides an alternative focus on the language used to develop characters or settings and how simile, metaphor and personification can engage the reader.

The following colour coding has been used to analyse the text:

noun groups and [adjectival clauses as part of a noun group]/participants

adjectival phrases as part of a noun group

verbal groups/processes

Prepositional phrases:

adverbial phrases/circumstances

Language features such as similes and metaphors and personification are in *italics*.

Table 2 Analysis of text and language features

Summary of the plot across the chapters		Example of language features from each chapter
1	Abel meets Blueback.	He fell back into the water with a cold crash. *A cloud of bubbles* swirled around him, clinging to his skin *like pearls*. Orange starfish and yellow plates of coral glowed from the deepest slopes where his mother was already gliding *like a bird*.
2	Abel and his mother can't find Blueback.	After breakfast Abel carried seaweed up to the fruit trees. He filled bags of washed kelp and heaved them up the slope from the jetty to the orchard.
3	Abel goes to school and daydreams.	He died when Abel was two years old but the bay and the garden and the house were *like a memory of him*.
4	Abel turns twelve and Macka dies.	*A cloud of gulls hung* over the two boats.
5	Abel goes to boarding school.	Home *throbbed* in him *like a headache*. Only in his sleep did Abel feel free. In his dreams *Blueback loomed up at him out of the blurry dark*.
6	Abel takes his boat out and watches the whales.	A foul mist rose over them and Abel saw the glistening backs of right whales all around.
7	Abel and his mum beat Costello.	He felt *like a speck, like a bubble* on the sea left by a breaking wave, here for a moment and then gone. Some days he sped close in to long *sugary* beaches. He stayed just behind the breakers and was showered with their spray and saw the great, strange land through *the wobbly glass of the waves*. He saw *the sun melting like butter* on white dunes.

8	Abel watches the tiger shark die and returns to school.	It sailed down into the black deep *like a torpedoed ship*. Abel went back to school in the new year feeling older, different. That summer he learnt that there was nothing in nature as cruel and savage as a greedy human being.
9	Abel goes to high school and his mother beats the developers.	It was love that stopped her from being lonely, that made her strong. It was *like food to her*. Abel knew that it was his mother's love [that kept him going] all those dull high school years while he was stuck inland, *holding his breath until he was blue* in the face.
10	The pilchards die.	'*The ocean is sick*,' said Abel's mother. 'Something's wrong.' It was a mystery. And the more he thought about it the more *the whole sea seemed to be a puzzle*. Abel wanted to figure it out.
11	Abel goes to university and meets his future wife Stella.	Abel Jackson went to university to figure out the sea. His mother smiled about that. *He'd lived* half his life underwater, *his best friend was a fish* and now he was leaving Longboat Bay to learn about the sea. It seemed a bit mad to her but she shrugged her shoulders and let him go.
12	Abel becomes a marine biologist.	*Blueback still swam through his dreams*.
13	Abel goes home.	*The sea grew tormented.* *Surf hammered the shore and chewed it away*. *Wind gusts screamed* till she covered her ears. Dora Jackson began writing letters...She wrote hundreds of them. They were *like a coral spawn*, *those letters, tiny white messages [that drifted out from Longboat Bay into the offices of people all over the country.]*
14	Baby Dora is born.	One cold winter night a baby was born at Longboat Bay. They called her Dora after her grandmother. Her fists were *like pink seashells* and *she cried like a bird*.
15	Dora dies.	*Her hair was white as the sand on the shore* and little Dora liked to feel it silky between her fingers.
16	Baby Dora meets Blueback.	*The smallest diver hung like a sail between the grownups* as they *flew down* to the rubbly bottom. Out of the shadows, from a crack in the reef, a huge blue creature *came swirling* at them. *The little girl's eyes grew big* in her mask and she *chirped* in her snorkel. But Blueback slipped *in close to them*, fins *rippling*. His scales shone. His tail fanned. *He was the colour of all their dreams* and he rested against the child, *quivering* with life.

Focus on language for expressing ideas and interacting with others

Figurative language is a tool used to express ideas in texts, particularly narratives. Hence, it plays a role in representing the field of a text. However, 'as writers use figurative language to enrich their writing and to present a "moment" in a fresh and stimulating way' (McDonald, 2013, p. 137), the choice of language can also be seen in relation to tenor and how such choices create an emotional response for the reader.

Simile, metaphor and personification are used by Tim Winton to paint word pictures for the reader. His choice of unusual words also helps to define the relationship with the reader, or the tenor of the text. The language for expressing ideas includes noun groups, verbal groups and prepositional phrases, both adjectival prepositional phrases which are included in noun groups and adverbial phrases which can be placed anywhere in the clause (see examples presented in Table 2). These language choices are used to develop the similes, metaphors and personification, which make the word pictures richly descriptive and emotive.

For example, Blueback provides a focal point throughout the text as he is a metaphor for the sea and the natural environment and the metaphor includes Abel whose life away from this environment meant that he held '*his breath until he was blue in the face.*' Here are some other instances: '*In his dreams Blueback loomed up at him out of the blurry dark … Blueback still swam through his dreams … Out of the shadows, from a crack in the reef, a huge blue creature came swirling at them … He was the colour of all their dreams and he rested against the child, quivering with life.*'

It is an obvious advantage to be able to draw on storytellers of Tim Winton's calibre to engage students and also to provide a fantastic model of the way language can be used to interact with a reader to provoke emotion and paint pictures with words. Stories are important in all our lives and at every stage of our lives.

> Stories are central genres in all cultures, in some form in almost every imaginable situation and stage of life. They are intimately woven into the minutiae of everyday life, whenever we come together. They are told in all social groupings to interpret life's chaos and rhythms, to evaluate each other's behaviour, and to educate and entertain our children. There is something miraculous about the way a child's attention is instantly drawn by a story, as their imagination is ignited and held. (Martin & Rose, 2008, p. 49)

The *Australian Curriculum: English* identifies the following content in Year 6 which can be addressed based on teacher preparation and knowledge about texts and language.

Language	Understand how authors often innovate on text structures and play with language features to achieve particular aesthetic, humorous and persuasive purposes and effects (ACELA1518)
	Understand how ideas can be expanded and sharpened through careful choice of verbs, elaborated tenses and a range of adverb groups/phrases (ACELA1523)
	Investigate how vocabulary choices, including evaluative language can express shades of meaning, feeling and opinion (ACELA1525)
Literature	Experiment with text structures and language features and their effects in creating literary texts, for example, using imagery, sentence variation, metaphor and word choice (ACELT1800)
Literacy	Plan, draft and publish imaginative, informative and persuasive texts, choosing and experimenting with text structures, language features, images and digital resources appropriate to purpose and audience (ACELY1714)

Supporting the learner

Before reading the novel students should be familiarised with the author, Tim Winton, and his interest in protecting marine environments. Depending on the students' independent reading either allow them to read the whole text at their own pace or choose to read sections with a class or group for the pleasure of reading and enjoying the story. Readers bring their own understandings to a text and this skilfully constructed text provides plenty of opportunities for readers to build bridges to the text either through their lived or literary experiences.

> But readers because they process the text are active agents in making meaning, which they do in the light of their own personal experience and subject position. Thus, they bring different perceptions to the text and their response will be governed by a variety of such factors. So each reader creates his or her own text, or "poems his own poem". (Saxby, 1997, p. 16)

The focus in this teaching and learning sequence (Figure 2) will be on this masterful use of language that can ignite and hold imagination and how young authors can learn to do this.

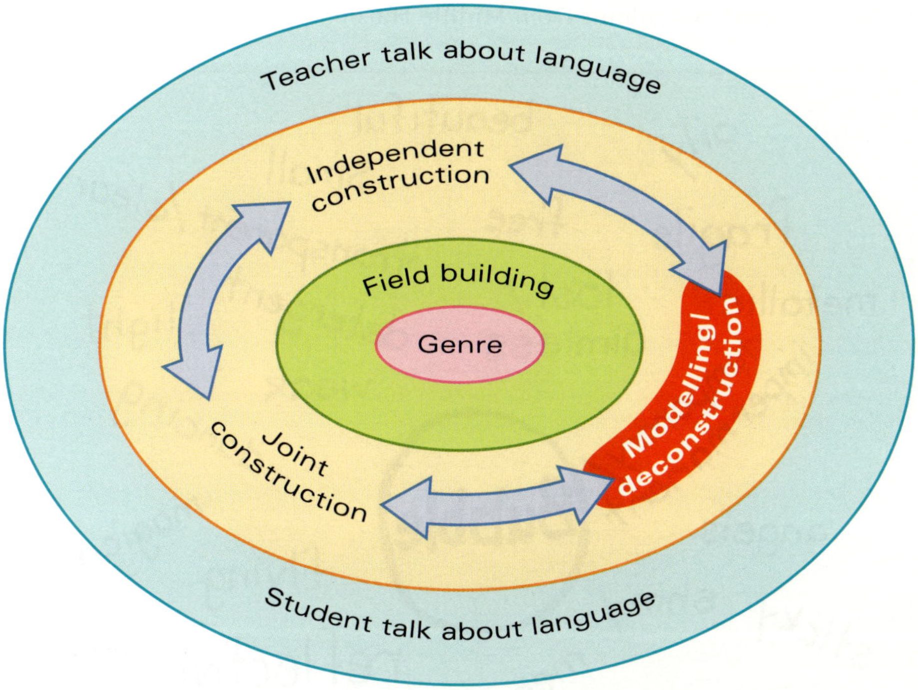

Figure 2
Adapted teaching and learning cycle with emphasis on deconstruction

Spotlight on language for expressing ideas and interacting with others during text deconstruction

Read a section of the text such as Chapter 7 and begin to develop students' understanding of the purpose of literary features by starting with **simile** then moving to **metaphor** and **personification**.

Using the examples from Chapter 7 as a starting point such as the sentence 'He felt *like a speck, like a bubble* on the sea left by a breaking wave, here for a moment and then gone' explicitly point to the use of the words *like* or *as*. These indicate that these similes are prepositional phrases which function as adverbial phrases of manner, answering the question 'How/In what way?' eg, '*like a speck, like a bubble*' or 'white *as the sand*'.

Provide students with bubble makers and allow them to blow bubbles and observe, photograph or draw them. Develop a word bank to describe the appearance of bubbles eg, *round, shiny, reflective*; and then their properties eg, *fragile, delicate, impermanent* (see Figure 3 for an example of a word bank developed by students from Middle Harbour Public School).

Figure 3
Bubble word bank

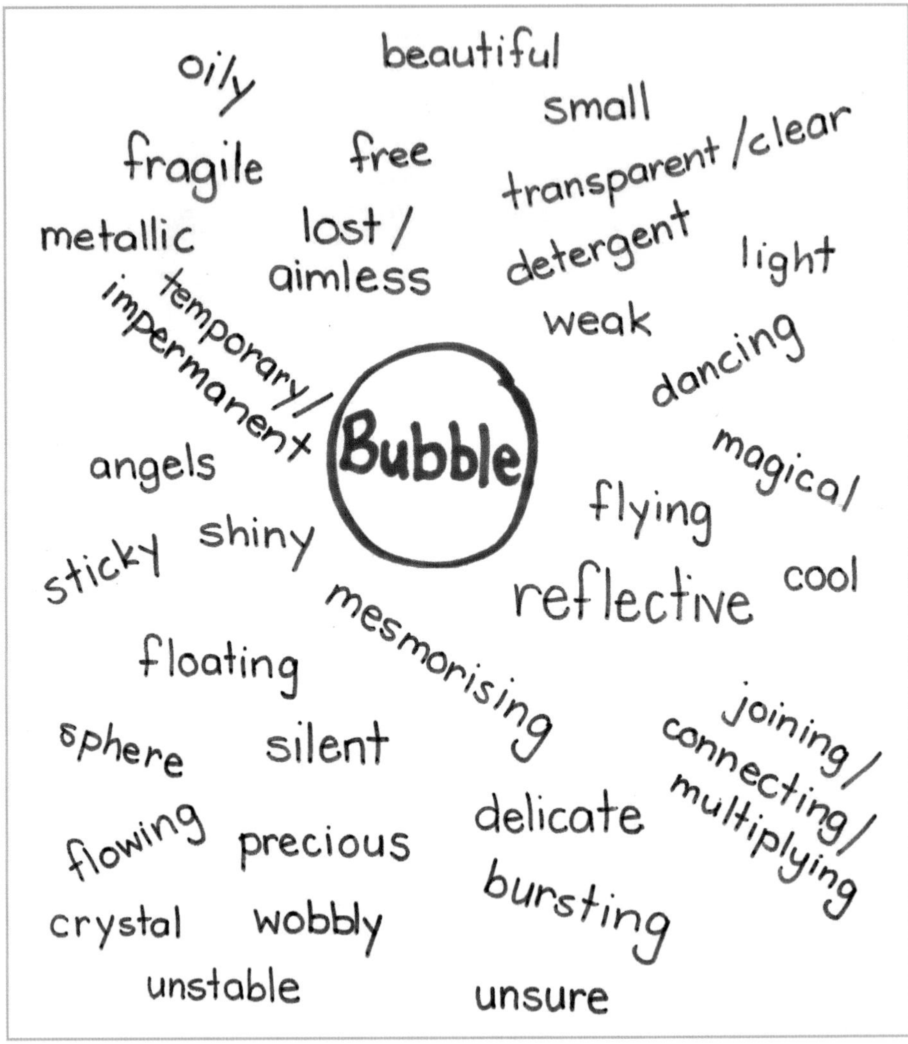

Return to examples of the simile from the text such as: '*a bubble on the sea left by a breaking wave*' and ask students to provide other examples of impermanence. Such as I feel like a: '*a snake shedding its skin; a storm passing through the night; a wave crashing in the sea; a feather fallen from a bird; a tear running down her face.*' (These are quotes from students of Middle Harbour Public School.)

Ask students to think about how the character of Abel feels if he is described as feeling like a 'bubble' or 'speck'. In pairs ask students to complete a thought cloud to show how Abel felt (see Figure 4). Repeat the process describing the appearance of the sea and the properties of the sea.

Figure 4
Sample of a thought cloud

Record and discuss suggestions in terms of emotions or feelings that they evoke in the reader. Not only do the language choices effectively describe the setting, the use of figurative language also establishes an interpersonal connection between the reader and the feelings and perceptions of the character. It is such choices which evoke feelings within reader.

The focus on similes is a useful starting point as it is more challenging for students to understand the concepts of metaphor and personification but they can be taught simultaneously by building on an understanding of the purpose and construction of a simile.

To explain metaphors to students, focus on the relating verb *to be* as the starting point of a metaphor and explain that a metaphor is the same as a simile but the words *like* or *as* are replaced by part of the verb to be: *am, are, is, was, were.*

For example in Chapter 13:

> *She (Dora)* ***is*** *part of the bay.*

> In Chapter 16:

> *He (Blueback)* ***was*** *the colour of all their dreams.*

Starting here students can change their own similes into metaphors, eg, 'He felt like a bubble' on the sea becomes 'He was a bubble on the sea.' After changing some of their own similes into metaphors ask students to consider the change of meaning. Use prompts to help students compare the intensification of feeling and which feature they consider is the most emotionally powerful.

To draw attention to personification, return to the text and look for the use of personification where metaphor has been used to personify. For example, in Chapter 10:

The ocean ***is*** *sick.*

The air ***roared*** *with flies.*

In Chapter 13:

The sea ***grew tormented****.*

Surf ***hammered*** *the shore and* ***chewed*** *it away.*

Wind gusts ***screamed*** *till she covered her ears.*

The actions of becoming sick or tormented and of roaring, hammering, chewing and screaming define the sea and the wind as in some way human with the ability to think and act.

Encourage one or two students to walk in role as one of the characters from the story and ask them to show in their walk an emotion that the character is expressing at that point of the text, for example, bravery, pride, happiness, sadness, curiousity, and homesickness. Tell the rest of the class which character is walking around their classroom and what has just happened in the text. A suggestion is: Abel has just left for school.

After the students have identified the emotion jointly construct a metaphor to describe the character. For example:

Bravery: *Abel* ***was*** *a lion.*

Happiness: *Abel* ***was*** *the first day of the school holidays.*

Sadness: *Abel* ***was*** *grey skies and drizzling rain.*

Using the word banks developed, ask students to construct some similes and metaphors to show how Abel felt. Use the text as a starting point:

He felt like 'a bubble on the sea left by a breaking wave'.

He felt like '*a sandcastle left on the beach* here for a moment and then gone'.

He felt like '*a feather, left behind from a flock of birds, attached for years* and then *simply* gone.'

(These are quotes from students of Middle Harbour Public School.)

Choose examples from other parts of the text to extend understandings and discussion of the use of the literary features.

Summary of a teaching and learning sequence

Building the field

- After reading the text investigate Tim Winton's background and environmental passion.
- Discuss the language used in one or more of the chapters and the work that Tim Winton is making the language do. For instance the examples of the prepositional phrases/circumstances of place (adverbial phrases) in Chapter 2 are used to describe Dora & Abel's home but the examples of circumstances of manner in Chapter 7 are similes to show how he felt or how the sun appeared on the dunes.

Text deconstruction

- Work with examples of language at work in describing characters and settings in the chapters so students are supported to identify the use of metaphor, simile and personification and how these help to evoke feelings in the reader.

Joint construction

- Jointly construct one of the scenes or chapters and use the language in the text as a starting point to help students develop their own metaphors or similes or to use personification to dramatise one aspect of the scene.

Independent construction

- Ask pairs or small groups to choose one scene they particularly like and using the examples from the text as a starting point, write that scene using their own words and using some of the literary features.

Resources

Winton, T 1997, *Blueback*. Pan Macmillan, Sydney.

The Wilderness Society, Tim Winton's Ningaloo Reef Rally Speech, viewed 19 March 2015, <https://www.wilderness.org.au/articles/tim-wintons-ningaloo-reef-rally-speech >.

World Wildlife Fund, 'Author Tim Winton on his love for the sea and our generation's opportunity to protect it', viewed 19 March 2015, <http://www.wwf.org.au/?4120/Author-Tim-Winton-on-his-love-for-the-sea-and-our-generations-opportunity-to-protect-it >.

Australian Marine Conservation Society, 'Author Tim Winton in Sydney to promote marine conservation', viewed 19 March 2015, <http://www.marineconservation.org.au/news.php/278/author-tim-winton-in-sydney-to-promote-marine-conservation)>.

section two

Writing in the informative world

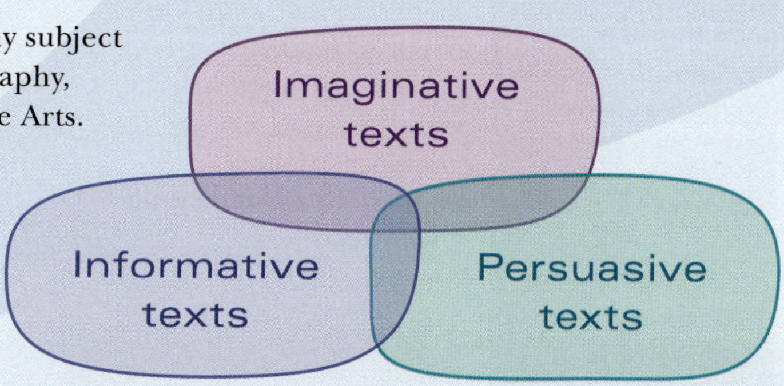

Writing informative texts occurs in many subject areas including Science, History, Geography, English, Personal Development and The Arts. The *Australian Curriculum: English* (2012) states that the primary purpose of informative texts is to provide information. 'They include texts which are culturally important in society and are valued for their informative content, as a store of knowledge and for their value as part of everyday life' (ACARA, 2012).

In this section, models of how to plan for and teach informative writing include:

When choosing informative texts in primary schools there is often a stronger focus on field or subject matter at the expense of tenor and mode. However 'the teacher's role is to design contexts and plan activities in all curriculum areas that provide opportunities for learners to develop the particular language they need in order to participate effectively in school.' (Derewianka & Jones, 2012, p. 9) We have therefore chosen modelled texts to support student writing, which provide information students are not only required to engage with but also compose within meaningful contexts. The reading and writing of informative texts serve as an apprenticeship into specialised subject areas.

Section two			
Writing in the informative world			
Subject	Science	Geography	History
Writing	Procedural recount/ experiment report	Comparative report	Historical recount
Reading	*Race some beads*	*The difference between the Amazon and Daintree rainforests*	*Aliens*
Language for expressing and connecting ideas	Action, perceiving and relating verbs/ processes, general and specific nouns/ participants, adverbials/ circumstances		Noun groups/ participants
Language for interacting with others			Vocabulary to convey perspective
Language for text structure and organisation		Word associations and conjunctions	
Spotlight on the teaching and learning cycle	Building the field	Joint construction (editing)	Independent writing

model one

Writing to recount scientifically

Writing	Procedural recount/experiment report
Reading	*Race some beads*
Language	Language for expressing ideas (action, perceiving and relating verbs/processes, general and specific nouns/participants, adverbials/circumstances)
Supporting the student	Building the field

The following teaching and learning sequence looks at the development of scientific writing and the key role of using oral language and hands-on experience to build the field in preparation for writing. The construction of an experiment report or procedural recount is an apprenticeship into the culture and thinking of the discipline of Science (Kalantzis and Cope, 2012).

> School science seeks to initiate the young into an understanding of scientific knowledge and scientific methods, and this has consequences for the scientific discourses that students learn to write, for it involves learning a technical language and a set of written text types or genres which encode scientific principles and procedures. (Christie & Derewianka, 2008, p. 149)

According to the *Australian Curriculum: Science* (ACARA, 2012), as well as developing 'Scientific understanding' and 'Knowledge of Science as a human endeavour', students need to be able to engage in 'Scientific inquiry'. This involves developing investigative questions, making predictions, planning and conducting investigations to answer questions, making and recording observations in a range of forms (eg, graphs and tables), using tools and materials safely, comparing results with predictions, discussing fairness in investigations and representing and communicating ideas through written texts (ACARA, 2012).

To address the requirements of the curriculum and in particular support writing, the context for this teaching and learning example is from the Physical Sciences. The focus of this model is on the concept that *Heat can be produced in many ways and can move from one object to another* (ACARA, 2012). Although students will be reading procedural texts they will be writing recounts of the procedures they conduct through the process of scientific inquiry.

In Science, students need to engage in and compose a range of oral, written and multimodal texts. When locating texts targeted at young learners in books and online for field building and modelling, it is not uncommon to find procedural texts on how to undertake investigations. In these typical texts, aspects of scientific inquiry, such as asking investigative questions, recording results and making generalisations, may be embedded implicitly (see Figure 1, Ardley, 2015, p. 32). When students learn to think and write like scientists the processes required for scientific inquiry need to be made explicit. Students need to understand the differences between procedural texts and procedural, or experiment recounts which accompany investigations at different points of Scientific Inquiry.

Figure 1
Procedural text with implicit aspects of scientific inquiry

Knowledge about texts and language

The following analysis shows the importance of linking language choices to the purpose of experiment reports/procedural recounts in the context of Science. Knowledge about such texts assists students in composing their own texts after engaging in scientific inquiry as shown in Table 1.

Table 1 Analysis of features of the procedural recount/experiment report

Context	The experiment report or procedural recount, based on 'Race some beads' (Figure 1), has been composed in the context of students having undertaken the particular experiment. 'Science in school recontextualises not only the scientific fields, but the genres with which they are associated' (Martin & Rose, 2008, p. 199). The text is context specific to the world of Science as it reflects and represents the thinking involved in 'doing' Science. School texts such as this one are appropriations of texts found in science and industry (Schleppegrell, 2004). This context requires both precise language in order to make sense of the world, as well as a method for scientists to document their work.
Social purpose/ genre	The social purpose of the procedural recount genre is informative, as the text informs through recounting the process of investigating. Due to its multiple stages, the purpose is 'to recount in order and with accuracy the aim, steps, results and conclusion of a scientific activity' (Unsworth, 2000, p. 250).
Field (What is the subject matter?)	The field of the text evolves across the stages. In the initial stages the specific naming of processes, objects and locations is conveyed through everyday language. In the later stages there is shift towards more general naming of phenomena in the move from undertaking actions to observing and drawing conclusions.
Tenor (Who is involved and what is the relationship?)	As is expected in scientific texts, there is no attitudinal expression as attention is placed on the importance of the phenomenon (Christie & Derewianka, 2008). With students inexperienced in scientific writing they may include the personal pronoun (eg, ***I** put the spoons in the beaker*) with the 'investigator' as the actor. However, as students develop scientific inquiry they can be guided towards writing in the passive voice (eg, *The spoons were placed into a beaker*) and remove the personal reference and shift emphasis to the scientific materials and concepts.
Mode (What is the channel of communication?)	In the modelled text (See Table 2) the questions support students in understanding the staging of the text which in effect act as headings. These along with the numbered steps within the method, organise the text and guide the reader. It is possible to also incorporate the use of images across the stages of the text. Language use is precise as the procedural recount is removed from the investigation context requiring the processes, materials and phenomena to be clearly named and developed across the text.

Text structure and phases	As is characteristic of a procedural recount the staging is very clear. The investigating question indicates the aim which reflects the scientific knowledge being negotiated. The method records the equipment used and processes conducted in the investigation. It should be noted that due to the purpose of the text, the steps in the procedure are written in past tense (Christie & Derewianka, 2008; Halliday & Martin, 1993) as the writing has occurred after the investigation. In a context where the experiment is done simultaneously, the method may be written in present tense and have an instructional rather than recount function. The results record observations that are interpreted in the conclusion which then relate back to the aim or investigating question. As students become more experienced they might also include stages focusing on safety and variability (ACARA, 2012). The phases within the stages are important for explicitly developing the function of each stage, particularly in the results and conclusion stage with a focus on shifting from the actions in the method to the specific observations and generalisations required in the later stages.

Understanding features of a modelled text

A close analysis of a procedural recount (Table 2) identifies features at the clause level and shows patterns within clauses and through the whole text which relate to the text achieving its purpose. This knowledge assists in developing a teaching sequence. The following colour coding has been used to analyse the text:

action verbs   sensing/perceiving verbs   **relating verbs**

Table 2 Analysis of text and language features of a procedural recount

Text structure	Phases	Experiment: *Race some beads*
Aim	Investigative question	What were we investigating?
		What happens to the bead and butter when we change the material of the spoons?
Method	Equipment and materials	*What did we need?* glass beaker hot water beads

		butter or margarine wooden spoon metal spoon plastic spoon
	Steps	*What did we do?* We stuck a bead onto the spoons with butter. We stood the spoons in a beaker. We poured hot water into the beaker.
Results	Observation	*What did we see?* We noticed that the metal spoon heated up faster. We observed that the butter melted and the bead on the metal spoon fell first.
Conclusion	Generalisation	*What did we find out?* Heat spreads better through some materials than others. Metal **is** a good conductor of heat and wood and plastics **are** poor conductors of heat.

Focus on language for expressing ideas

The field of a text relates to the ideas expressed by a writer. Of particular importance in a scientific report or procedural recount are ideas expressed through the participants/noun groups, processes/verb groups and circumstances/adverbials at clause level. The development of scientific thinking unfolds through these choices and is reflected throughout the stages and phases of the text.

In looking closely at the process/verb choices in the text, the choices clearly reflect the function of each stage/phase. By focusing on such features the purpose of the text can be discussed at the text, stage, phase, clause and group/word level. As the text unfolds the processes/verbs shift from action verbs in the method to sensing, in particular, perceiving verbs in the results stage and relating verbs in the conclusion stage. Similarly the participants are named using specific nouns which then become generalised and technical (eg, *conductors*). Notice that scientific generalisations are made in the conclusion stage of the text. In the steps phase there is frequent use of adverbials of place which are important in conducting the actual experiment. As the text progresses the shift is to adverbials of time and manner, as observations are made and conclusions drawn about how phenomena occur (see Table 3). The following colour coding has been used in the table:

verb/process
noun/participant
adverbial/circumstance

Table 3 Deconstruction of language choices in a procedural recount

Text stage	Verb/process			Noun/participant		Adverbial/ circumstance
	Action	**Perceiving**	**Relating**	**Specific**	**General**	**Time/place/ manner**
Method	stuck stood poured			bead butter spoons beaker hot water		onto the spoons with butter in a beaker into the beaker
Results	melted fell	noticed observed		the metal spoon the butter the bead the metal spoon		faster first
Conclusion	spread		is are		heat materials metal wood plastics conductors of heat	better through some materials than others

The *Australian Curriculum: English* (ACARA, 2012) identifies the following content in Year 3 which can be addressed based on teacher preparation and knowledge about experiment reports or procedural recount texts requiring the scientific thinking and language.

Language	Understand how different types of texts vary in use of language choices, depending on their purpose and context (for example, tense and types of sentences) (ACELA1478)
	Understand that verbs represent different processes, for example doing, thinking, saying, and relating and that these processes are anchored in time through tense (ACELA1482)
Literacy	Plan, draft and publish imaginative, informative and persuasive texts demonstrating increasing control over text structures and language features and selecting print and multimodal elements appropriate to the audience and purpose (ACELY1682)

Supporting the learner

Based on teacher knowledge about experiment reports/procedural recounts and associated language choices, the following teaching and learning sequence outlines steps to support students in developing scientific inquiry to ultimately support writing their own texts.

It is critical that induction into the scientific world is developed through initially building field knowledge and communicating orally around hands-on experiences (Honig, 2010). As models of experimental reports/procedural recount texts are not often found in scientific texts targeted at young learners, texts used for field building and engaging in scientific inquiry may differ to those used for modelling, joint and independent construction. For this reason the texts students read are more likely to be procedural rather than procedural recounts.

Spotlight on language for expressing ideas during field building

In this detailed example of building the field (see Figure 2), focus is placed on developing scientific inquiry as students are 'being' scientists through hands-on activities and oral language development. This way of thinking and development of language is crucial for supporting the move into writing scientifically.

Figure 2
Adapted teaching and learning cycle with emphasis on field building

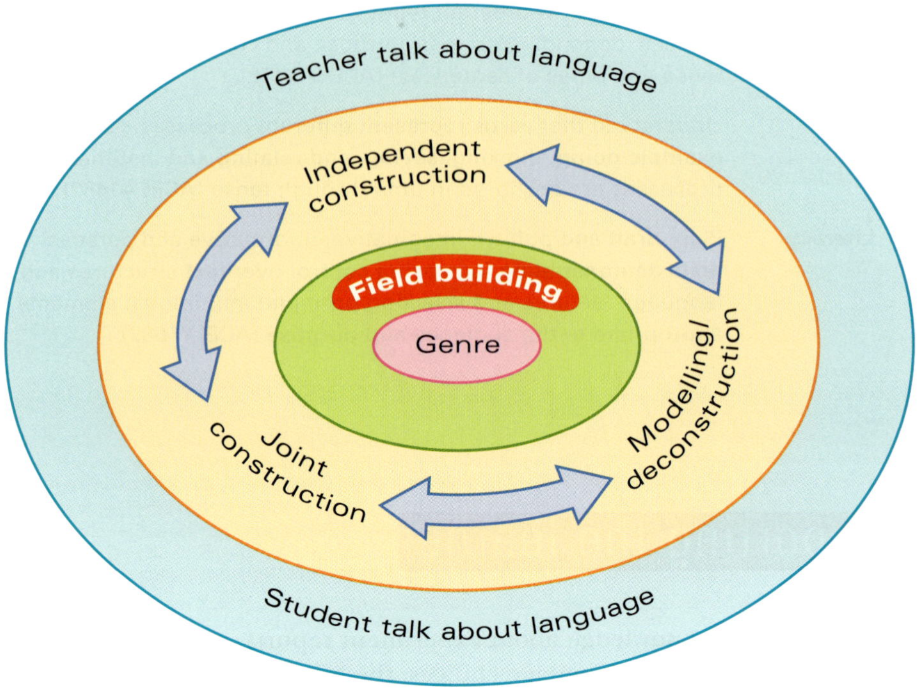

In reading and enacting experimental procedures students need to be involved in face-to-face interactions. When interacting through hands-on activities it may be that objects, let alone concepts, or ways of thinking do not need to be explicitly named as the language is embedded within the context (Gibbons, 2002). Due to this, moving straight from an experiment to writing can mean that scientific knowledge, language and thinking have not yet been developed or made explicit. By building the field prior to conducting experiments students are positioned to make informed predictions or hypotheses (Honig, 2010). Further oral interaction after conducting experiments, prior to writing, ensures that students are well supported to shift into writing scientifically.

In introducing the topic create a Wordle (Feinberg, 2008) based on key terms associated with the topic. It should include both familiar and unfamiliar terms (see Figure 3). Students can predict what the topic will be about and the terms can be used as a reference throughout the teaching cycle.

Display images (Figure 4) associated with the topic and brainstorm ideas on sticky notes. This may involve recycling terms from the Wordle that was created. Sort the sticky notes into everyday or scientific terms. These can also be used to create semantic webs as the topic progresses.

Figure 3
Example of a Wordle

Figure 4
Images supporting the brainstorming of heat transfer

Read a range of texts with students including books, images and videos. Prior to each reading provide the title or associated image and ask students to complete a KWL chart – K(What I already KNOW) and W (What I WANT to know) L (What I have LEARNT).

After reading each text students complete the **L** section. Any new terms can be added to semantic webs. These strategies assist with finding out what students know and tapping in to their background knowledge. They also reveal the everyday and or more specialised language they may have or require (Derewianka & Jones, 2012). With this prior knowledge, once students get to the hands-on activities such as experiments, they will be better prepared to make informed predictions as opposed to guesses based on limited or everyday knowledge (Honig, 2010).

At this point conduct experiments with students which include reading procedural texts and completing hands-on tasks in small groups. Also, encourage students to photograph the steps, as these can be used to support writing after the completion of experiments. In the context of each experiment orally develop investigating questions (see the extract from Primary Connections (2011. p. 64), that shows the process for developing investigative questions). A focus on developing investigative questions apprentices students into scientific thinking (Kalantzis & Cope, 2012).

> All science investigations involve variables. Variables are things that can be changed, measured or kept the same (controlled) in an investigation.
>
> - The independent variable is the thing that is changed during the investigation.
> - The dependent variable is the thing that is affected by the independent variable, and is measured or observed.
>
> An example of the way students can structure questions for investigation is:
> What happens to ______________ when we change ______________?
> *dependent variable* *independent variable*
> (Australian Academy of Science (2011), Melting Moments, Year 3, Chemical sciences)

It is beneficial to have groups conduct a range of experiments so there is a context for sharing what they did and what they found out. The following resources, details of which are at the end of this model, provide related experiments:

- Primary Connections, Melting Moments, Year 3, Chemical Sciences
- Science Web Australia, Unit 1, Transfer of Heat
- Technology Tom, Conductors and Spoons
- ACARA, Year 3 Science Portfolios

After conducting experiments a focus on talking and listening is critical. Teacher knowledge of the mode continuum (Martin, 1985) can guide classroom talk to shift student language from everyday/spoken-like choices towards context specific written-like choices in the scientific context. Talk serves as the bridge between hands-on 'doing' to writing.

Once groups conduct their own experiments, the teacher can explicitly introduce key terms such as *materials, heat* and *conductor* by attaching these terms to what occurred in the investigations. Then, as ideally each group undertakes a different experiment, they can report back to the class. This serves as an information gap activity as each group reports on their own particular experience. This creates an authentic need for sharing findings (Gibbons, 2002). When students are discussing their experiences the teacher needs to use careful questioning and responses to develop a more equitable, conversational style in the classroom which guides students towards the more scientific structures and vocabulary. During this process teacher-guided reporting positions students to move towards more scientific discourse due to teacher scaffolding while also making sense of the experience (Gibbons, 2002). This differs from the Initiation-Response-Evaluation patterns that are common in classrooms (Edwards-Groves, Anstey & Bull, 2014). Appropriate strategic questioning guides students from recounting procedures to generalising and drawing conclusions.

This is the critical point where the teacher needs to be aware of the groups' requirements at certain points in writing a procedural recount. The teacher can then give guidance with regard to language structures for the participants, processes and circumstances through oral language.

Such concept and language development in the context of scientific inquiry, ensures students are prepared to participate in constructing procedural recounts. The move to actually writing the recount represents a shift from the action and talk undertaken at the stage of conducting experiments. Once the field is built before and after reading and conducting procedures, students can be supported through text deconstruction, joint and independent construction.

Summary of a teaching and learning sequence

Building the field

- Create a Wordle to display key terms on the topic.
- Brainstorm and classify terminology and develop semantic webs.
- Read a range of texts and complete KWL charts.
- Conduct and photograph a range of experiments, focusing on investigating questions.
- Students report on experiments while language is developed through teacher-guided reporting.

Text deconstruction/modelled reading

- After reading a range of procedures and conducting experiments display examples of procedural recounts and discuss purpose and function of each stage.
- Compare features of a procedure with a procedural recount discussing their use at points during scientific inquiry. Note how this changes the tense chosen.
- In a model of a procedural recount identify verb/process choice across the text. Classify as action, sensing/perceiving, relating processes/verbs (See Derewianka, 2011 and Humphrey, Droga & Feez, 2012) and relate to where each type occurs within the stages and phases of the text. Point out the use of past tense (Table 2). Discuss how scientists move from doing to observing to describing/generalising and this is reflected in text structure and verb choice.
- List participants or ideas as specific or general and also link to stages (Table 2). Discuss how the naming of 'things' in Science moves from the specific to more general ideas or phenomena.
- Identify adverbials across the text and how they tell detail about time, place and manner. Point out how this changes more to manner in the latter stages of the text (Table 3).

- Students assemble stages of the text, match to labels for stages/phases and identify participants, processes and circumstances.

Joint construction

- After conducting a particular experiment plan for writing a procedural recount. Recall the purpose and language choices discussed by referring to Table 2.
- Display images of the equipment and steps involved in the initial experiment.
- Display the question prompts for each stage of the text. Support students in constructing an investigating question (Primary Connections, 2011).
- As a whole class construct the equipment and method stages focusing attention on the specific participants, past tense action verbs and adverbials/circumstances surrounding the actions in the method.
- Continue joint writing by focusing on the perceiving verbs in the results and relating verbs in the conclusion as well as the shift to nouns for naming phenomena rather than specific objects and adverbial choices.
- After writing colour code the verb choices in the text and ask students to check if the text and each stage is achieving its purpose.

Independent construction

- After conducting other experiments on the topic students write their own procedural recounts. Depending on the needs of the students support can be provided through writing in small groups, focusing on one stage at a time, providing images for support, displaying sample texts and table of language features (Table 2), providing guiding questions, including sentence stems particularly for the results and conclusion stages. The Year 3 Science Portfolios indicate expectations in conducting and writing about investigations (ACARA, 2012).

Resources

Ardley, N 2015, *101 Great science experiments*, Dorling Kindersley, London.

Australian Academy of Science 2011, 'Primary Connections Melting Moments, Year 3, Chemical sciences', viewed 7 April 2015, <http://www.scootle.edu.au/ec/viewing/S5687/index.html >.

Feinberg, J 2008, Wordle, viewed 7 April 2015, < http://www.wordle.net >.

ReadWriteThink, 'K-W-L Chart', viewed 7 April 2015,<http://www.readwritethink.org/classroom-resources/printouts/chart-a-30226.html >.

Science Web Australia, 'Years 3-4 Unit 1 Transfer of Heat', viewed 7 April 2015, <http://scienceweb.asta.edu.au/years-3-4/unit1/lesson-two/yr34-unit1-lesson-two.html >.

Technology Tom, *Conductors*, viewed 7 April 2015, <http://www.technologytom.com/html/conductors.html>.

Technology Tom, *Spoons*, viewed 7 April 2015, <http://www.technologytom.com/html/spoons.html >.

ACARA, 2012, 'Year 3 Science Portfolios', viewed 7 April 2015, <http://www.australiancurriculum.edu.au/science/curriculum/f-10?layout=1#level3 >.

model two

Writing to compare entities

Writing	Comparative report
Reading	*The difference between the Amazon and Daintree rainforests*
Language	Language for creating cohesion: word associations and conjunctions
Supporting the student	Joint construction (editing)

This teaching and learning sequence was developed in the context of teaching Geography. The writing focus is on writing comparative reports comparing geographic features of countries in different continents such as Australia, Africa and South America. This requires knowledge about countries located in similar climate zones and their natural vegetation. This is addressed within the context of 'knowing and understanding how the Earth sustains all life' (ACARA, Year 4, 2015).

In this example, the text deconstruction is based on a comparative report comparing the features of the Daintree and Amazon rainforests. Knowledge about text and language is then applied to writing a comparison of the Kalahari Desert in Africa and the Great Victoria Desert in Australia.

Much field knowledge is required to compose such texts in terms of locating and organising information and features on a number of countries. Students can obtain information on environmental entities through many websites. However, accessible models of comparative reports tend to occur on travel sites or sites which share research across communities (eg, wikispaces, eHow, answers.com, prezi, etc). These types of sites support developing field knowledge and serve as an induction into geographical thinking. They also provide models for discussing text structures and features of a range of informational texts and can be used as a medium for publishing and sharing research. Examples of some such sites for investigating forms of comparison of these rainforests are included in the Resources section of this model.

It should be noted that when engaging with the field in order to locate facts, many visual sources such as graphs, tables, photographs and a variety of maps are useful for gathering geographical information.

Knowledge about texts and language

Choices for using the comparative report on geographical features of the Daintree and Amazon rainforests have been based on close analysis of text features (see Table 1); and particularly on how these features coherently organise information.

Table 1 Analysis of features of the comparative report

Context	The text *The difference between the Amazon and Daintree rainforests* is found on the eHow website. This site provides a range of articles of varying types written by freelance writers. In the broad culture, texts such as those found on sites like eHow can serve as an induction into a field of study. Such texts, which categorise and compare, represent a western way of viewing and communicating about the world (Derewianka & Jones, 2012). These sites allow for the sharing of accessible information and language where individuals share their own research. In saying this, they also provide the opportunity for critical reading and for checking the validity and accuracy of content within the culture of sharing information in various modes.
Social purpose/ genre	The purpose of a comparative report is to compare or contrast characteristics of similar entities (Derewianka & Jones, 2012, p. 175). In this case, the entities are the Amazon rainforest and the Daintree rainforest.
Field (What is the subject matter?)	The text *The difference between the Amazon and Daintree rainforests* contains some complex structures. For example, expanded noun groups serve to pack in information (eg, *a similar number of primitive plant families*). These build description and comparison of the two rainforests. The density of description may mean that some students need assistance when reading. This also reveals that building the field knowledge is required when engaging with and composing such texts.

	The noun groups contain the technical language one would expect to find in the geographical subject area, eg, *continents, borders, species*. Several noun groups also contain comparing adjectivals, eg, *more, similar*. Due to the dominance of description there is frequent use of relating verbs (eg, *is, has, contains*), as they link information by identifying and describing.
Tenor (Who is involved and what is the relationship?)	The texts contain little attitudinal meaning as the focus is on facts rather than opinion. However, there is evidence of some evaluative language, particularly in the general classification with vocabulary such as *essential, wonder* and *important* used to communicate the value of the two entities.
Mode (What is the channel of communication?)	The purpose of the text is achieved through written-like language choices through the careful organisation of information across sentences, paragraphs and the whole text. Meaning is developed across the text particularly through the use of word associations related to the language of comparison, resulting in a cohesive and coherent text (Derewianka, 2011).
Text structure and phases	Both the 'Title' and 'General Classification' introduce the entities to be compared. In the entity phase the two rainforests are classified as *ecological wonders* and then the sub category of *environmental categorisation* is introduced. The description stage of the text is divided into particular phases reflective of the geographical context and field. It is worth noting that 'common stages of a genre may be found across different fields, but phases within each stage are more likely to vary from field to field and text to text' (Martin & Rose, 2008, p. 142). Each paragraph addresses similarities and differences with regards to location and size followed by biodiversity. The structure is also supported by the use of subheadings.

Understanding features of a modelled text

The analysis of *The difference between the Amazon and Daintree rainforests* presented in Table 2 reveals the role of text and language features in creating cohesion and assists in developing a teaching sequence. The following colour coding has been used to analyse the text:

comparing adjectivals

intensifiers

conjunctions

Table 2 Analysis of text and language features

Stages	Phases	*The difference between the Amazon and Daintree rainforests*
Title		*The difference between the Amazon and Daintree rainforests*
General statement	Introduction of entities	Essential to our planet's health is the health of our rainforests. Two such ecological wonders, the Amazon and the Daintree rainforests, are similar in environmental categorisation but distinct from one another in some important ways.
Description	Similarities and differences in location	**Location** While the Amazon and Daintree are each confined to one continent – the Amazon to South America, and the Daintree to Australia – the Amazon exists within the borders of eight different countries and one international territory. Brazil, Bolivia, Peru, Colombia, Ecuador, Guyana, Suriname, Venezuela, and French Guiana all have part of the Amazon within their borders.
	Differences in size	**Size** The Amazon rainforest, despite logging and other threats that have reduced its size and continue to do so, covers an area of approximately 4.1 million square miles. The Daintree is **significantly** smaller, covering an area of approximately 750 square miles.
	Similarities and differences in biodiversity	**Biodiversity** The Daintree and Amazon both contain a similar number of primitive plant families. The Daintree contains 12 of 19 such plant families, impressive considering Daintree's **comparatively** small size. The Daintree also has more plant species with primitive features than any other tropical rainforest worldwide.

Focus on language for creating cohesive texts

The written-like cohesive mode of the text is achieved through many features including word associations or lexical cohesion (See Derewianka, 2011 and Humphrey, Droga & Feez, 2012). The way words are tied together across the text through the linking of meaning is particularly evident through the choice of words/groups for building comparison.

These words are primarily comparing adjectivals and **intensifiers** as well as conjunctions as seen in the highlighted words presented from the text in Table 3. The use of the words *both* and *each* are useful in building comparison as they mostly act as pronouns for talking about common features of the two entities simultaneously.

Table 3 Words for building cohesion in a comparative report

	Same	Different
adjectivals	similar in environmental categorisation a similar number of primitive plant families	distinct from one and other in some important ways **significantly** smaller **comparatively** small size more plant species with primitive features than any other tropical rainforest worldwide
conjunctions	while	but despite

These cohesive choices are also reflected in the staging and phasing of the text as the comparison develops, as depicted in Figure 1. In most phases of the description the paragraph begins with describing similarities and then moves on to describing the differences or aspects particular to one of the entities. Without the interspersing of these words for comparison across the text it would not achieve its purpose as effectively and would lack cohesion.

The *Australian Curriculum: English* identifies the following content in Year 4 which can be addressed based on teacher preparation and knowledge about comparative reports and their language features.

Language	Understand how texts vary in complexity and technicality depending on the approach to the topic, the purpose and the intended audience (ACELA1490)
	Understand how texts are made cohesive through the use of linking devices including pronoun reference and text connectives (ACELA1491)
Literacy	Reread and edit for meaning by adding, deleting or moving words or word groups to improve content and structure (ACELY1695)

Figure 1 Comparative language across stages and phases

Stage	Phase		Ecological wonders: Amazon	Ecological wonders: Daintree
General classification	Introduction of entities	**same/ similar**	environmental categorisation (rainforests)	
		different/ distinct		
Description	Similarities and differences in location	**same/ similar**	confined to one continent	
		different/ distinct	South America ... borders of eight different countries and one international territory (Brazil, Bolivia, Peru, Colombia, Ecuador, Guyana, Suriname, Venezuela, and French Guiana)	Australia
Description	Differences in size	**same/ similar**		
		different/ distinct	... an area of approximately 4.1 million square miles	... an area of approximately 750 square miles
Description	Similarities and differences in biodiversity	**same/ similar**	... a similar number of primitive plant families	
		different/ distinct		... 12 of 19 such plant families, impressive considering Daintree's **comparatively** small size. ... more plant species with primitive features than any other tropical rainforest

Supporting the learner

Based on teacher knowledge about text features and language, the following teaching and learning sequence (see Figure 2) outlines steps to support students in developing comparative reports on geographic features of countries across continents located in similar climate zones. The focus on cohesive devices supports the cohesion and organisation of the text.

There is a range of report genres including descriptive, classifying and comparative reports (Derewianka & Jones, 2012). When teaching students to construct comparative reports, knowledge of other types of reports would be a prerequisite. This background would allow for discussion about how the complexity of describing can differ.

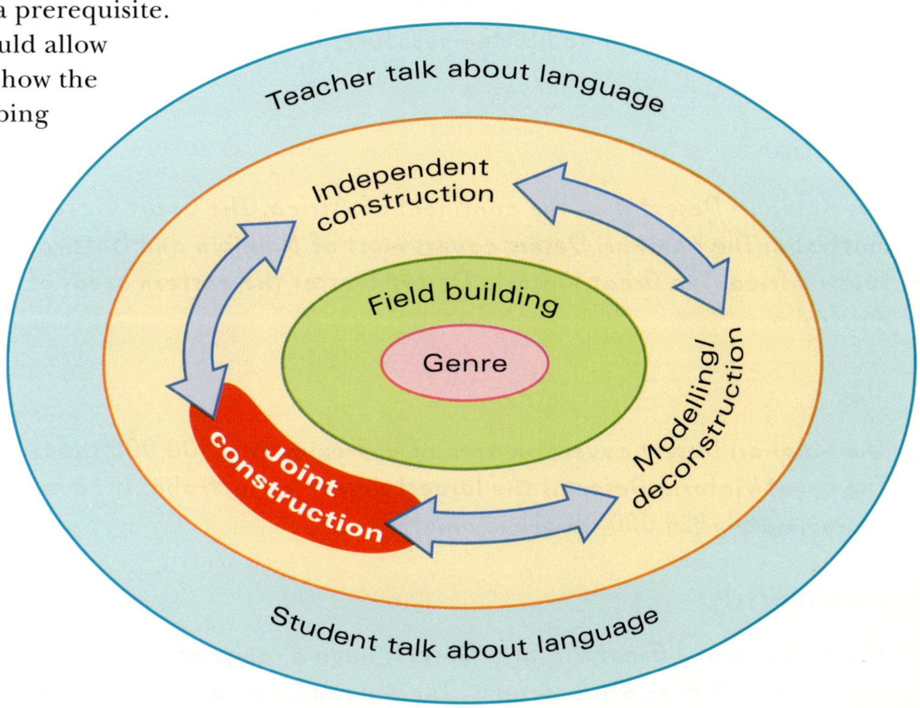

Figure 2
Adapted teaching and learning cycle with emphasis on joint construction

Spotlight on language for creating cohesion during joint construction/editing

In the detailed example that follows, the focus is on joint construction at the point of editing. The emphasis is on how to rework a text after a first draft paying attention to cohesive devices.

Display a draft of a comparative report on, *The difference between the Kalahari Desert and the Great Victoria Desert*, as shown in Figure 3. As the students have built and recorded much field knowledge about the topic of the two rainforests in the text deconstruction stage, the focus for joint construction should differ from the topic already addressed. Ensure that the draft text needs editing in regards to cohesive devices.

Figure 3
Draft comparative description

The Difference between the Kalahari and Great Victoria Deserts

Deserts are important to all life as they have their own ecosystem. The Kalahari Desert is a subtropical semi arid desert. The Great Victoria Desert is a subtropical semi arid desert. They have warm to hot temperatures in summer and cool temperatures in winter.

Location

The Kalahari Desert is on the continent of Africa. The Great Victoria Desert is in Australia. The Kalahari Desert covers most of Namibia and Botswana and parts of South Africa. The Great Victoria Desert crosses the eastern areas of Western and South Australia.

Size

The Kalahari Desert covers an area of approximately 900 000 square kilometres. The Great Victoria Desert is the largest desert in Australia. It covers an area of approximately 424 000 square kilometres.

Biodiversity

The Kalahari and Great Victoria Deserts have a range of wildlife because of their higher rainfall than other deserts. The Kalahari contains animals that have adapted to extreme hot and cold including the oryx, lions, leopards and cheetahs. The Great Victoria Desert has marsupials and a range of reptiles. They have significant vegetation particularly after rainfall. The Kalahari has over 400 species of plant life including grasses, scattered trees and shrubs. The Great Victoria Desert is scattered with large gum and oak trees and grasslands. In spring many wildflowers can be seen in the range of shrubs.

Support the students in discussing whether the text achieves its purpose. Discuss if there are any issues with the actual information in the text or if it is the cohesive devices that effect the text achieving its purpose.

Refer to the word webs shown in Figure 4, that should be developed during text deconstruction and revise the types of words which help develop comparison in a text. Ensure the word webs displaying cohesive devices are visible so that students can draw on the models from the deconstructed texts.

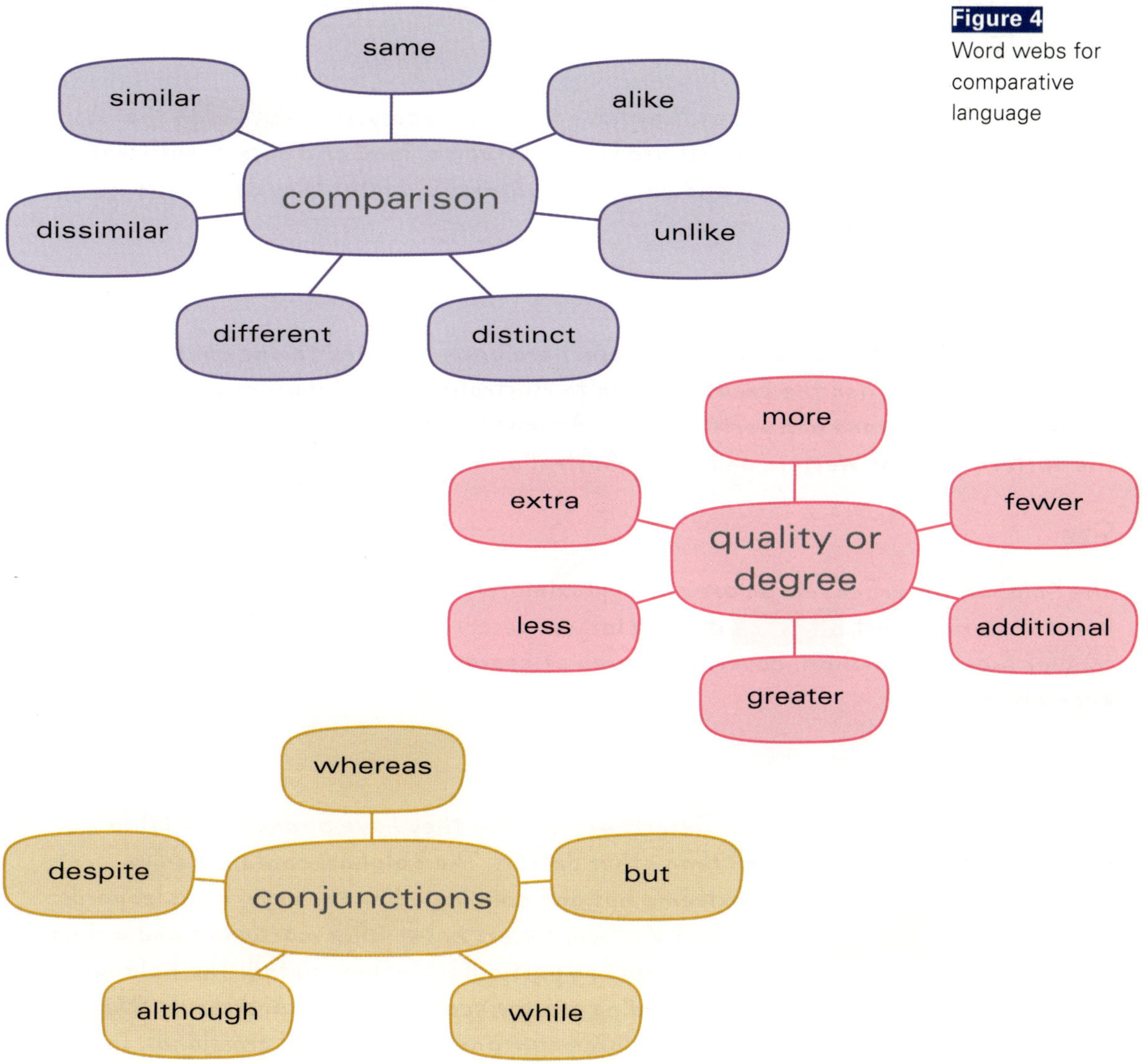

Figure 4 Word webs for comparative language

Jointly rework the text with particular focus on the use of conjunctions and comparative adjectives. Ensure the choices are constantly linked back to the purpose of the text and the role of the choices across the stages and phases. Editing and reworking of the text occurs as the teacher hands over the process to students. Students can be given mini whiteboards to record conjunctions or comparative adjectives. Students can hold up their choice for the class to see leading to a discussion about the most appropriate

Figure 5 Reviewed comparative description

The difference between the Kalahari and Great Victoria Deserts

Deserts are important to all life as they have their own ecosystem. Although the Kalahari and Great Victoria Deserts are both subtropical semi arid deserts with warm to hot temperatures in summer and cool temperatures in winter they do have some significant differences.

Location

While the Kalahari and Great Victoria Desert are each confined to one continent, the Kalahari to Africa, and the Great Victoria to Australia, the Kalahari covers most of Namibia and Botswana and parts of South Africa. The Great Victoria Desert crosses the eastern areas of Western and South Australia.

Size

The Kalahari Desert covers an area of approximately 900 000 square kilometres. The Great Victoria desert, although it is the largest desert in Australia, is significantly smaller than the Kalahari, covering an area of approximately 424 000 square kilometres.

Biodiversity

The Kalahari and Great Victoria Deserts are alike as they have a range of wildlife because of their higher rainfall than other deserts. The Kalahari contains larger animals that have adapted to extreme hot and cold including the oryx, lions, leopards and cheetahs. In contrast the Great Victoria Desert has smaller marsupials and a range of reptiles. Both have significant vegetation particularly after rainfall. The Kalahari has over 400 species of plant life including grasses, scattered trees and shrubs while the Great Victoria Desert is scattered with large gum and oak trees and grasslands. In spring many wildflowers can be seen in the range of shrubs.

choice coming from the students rather than the teacher (Rossbridge & Rushton, 2014). The first draft of the text can be reworked electronically if it is displayed and a cordless keyboard is available. A cordless keyboard can be passed around the class so that students have an opportunity to 'share the keyboard' and thus encourage more joint construction rather than modelled writing.

After writing highlight the cohesive devices and evaluate their role by comparing the text of the first draft (Figure 3) to the edited version (Figure 5).

Discussion during the process of joint editing is dependent on the field knowledge developed in earlier lessons, as well as the metalanguage taken on at the point of deconstruction.

Summary of a teaching and learning cycle

Building the field

- Use a globe and Google Earth to identify the continents of Australia, South America and Africa. Record countries within the continents on a map.
- View map of the world in the MapMaker Interactive (National Geographic) and display climate zones. Students can predict the type of environment and climate that might exist across the continents and what type of life might be found. Point out countries and regions located at similar latitudes.
- Place a piece of string around the globe and identify places which may have the same climate zone based on their latitude and particularly the equator and arctic poles.
- Locate possible places that might be similar and record on cards. Search for pictures showing what each place might look like.
- Classify into types of vegetation/environment, eg, rainforests, deserts, alpine, grasslands, tundra etc.

- Watch videos and read a range of texts on the range of places and vegetation.
- Using the Venn diagrams, Prezi or Popplet programs, record information on two places to show how they are similar or different, eg, Amazon and Daintree Rainforest/Kalahari and Great Victoria Desert, Andes and Snowy Mountains. This information can also be organised into a table as in Figure 1.
- Compare facts from different sources and investigate the authority of the authors.

Text deconstruction/modelled reading

- Read examples of descriptive reports on the Amazon and Daintree Rainforests.
- Display the text *The difference between the Amazon and Daintree Rainforests* and ask the students to identify how it differs from the descriptive reports.
- Discuss the purpose and intended audience and who would write such a text.
- Identify stages and phases and note how the stages are similar to descriptive reports but the phases differ due to the comparison of entities. In small groups students can categorise paragraphs from both descriptive and comparative reports and begin to identify differences in language features.
- Model highlighting words which build the comparison and link features of the two entities together. Discuss the relationship to the text stages and phases.
- Categorise the cohesive devices in a table (refer to Table 3). Students might repeat this with another comparative report, eg, The difference between the Andes Mountain Range in South America and the Snowy Mountains in Australia, and add additional words to the table.
- Create word webs to display word groups which make links across the text (refer to Figure 4).

Joint construction

- Display a draft comparative report which requires editing for cohesive devices.
- Draw on word webs to jointly rework the text through use of comparative adjectives and conjunctions.
- Highlight and evaluate the use of cohesive devices to compare the draft with the reworked text.

Independent construction

- Based on information recorded on the Venn diagrams, Prezi or Popplet programs, students select two places to compare. From a Venn diagram or Popplet students might represent their information and publish on Prezi to plan for writing.
- From this information students draft their own text either individually or in pairs.
- Students highlight their use of comparing adjectives, intensifiers and conjunctions that help the text achieve the purpose of comparing. Encourage students to check that these features are present across the whole text.
- Students redraft their text with a focus on cohesive devices.
- In small groups students share their texts and discuss the changes they have or have not made.
- Students can then make any further changes based on peer feedback and publish in school blogs, wikispaces or other sites where knowledge is shared in a community.

Resources

Answers.com, 'What are the differences between the Daintree and Amazon rainforests?', viewed 20 April 2015, http://www.answers.com/Q/What_are_the_differences_between_the_daintree_and_Amazon_rainforests >.

eHow, 'The differences between the Amazon and Daintree rainforests', viewed 20 April 2015, <http://www.ehow.com/facts_7213839_difference-between-amazon-daintree-rainforests.html >.

Prezi, 'Rainforests around the world!', viewed 20 April 2015, <https://prezi.com/ekacoy-lyqnn/rainforests-around-the-world/>.

MapMaker, 'Interactive Climate Zones', viewed 20 April, <http://mapmaker.education.nationalgeographic.com/?lg=11&b=1&f=131&bbox=-174.77644%2C11.95335%2C-8.13581%2C68.81593&ar_a=1&t=1&ls=000000001000>.

Notion Inc Popplet App, viewed 20 April 2015, <https://itunes.apple.com/us/app/popplet/id374151636?mt=8 >.

Wikispaces, 'Similarities and difference between the Daintree and Amazon Rainforests', viewed 20 April 2015' <http://hc-sk-daintree-amazon.wikispaces.com/similarities+and+differences>.

model three

Writing to recount historical perspectives

Writing	Historical recount
Reading	*Aliens*
Language	Language for expressing ideas and interacting with others: noun groups (participants), vocabulary for conveying perspective
Supporting the student	Independent writing

Through the integration of English and History content, historical literature, whose primary purpose is to inform, can be used to engage with historical skills and concepts. In this teaching context, Year 5 and 6 students can investigate 'perspective and interpretations' (ACARA, 2012) when responding to a range of texts and composing their own.

When working with a particular group of students, in order to tap into their prior knowledge, the content focus was on 'First contacts'. The students had studied this topic in the previous year. Having background knowledge allowed for a close focus on language choices and critical thinking about how perspective is conveyed through sources within an historical field. The *Australian Curriculum: History* (ACARA, 2012) suggests that students should be involved in both examining a range of sources and in the construction of a range of texts stating, 'Historical texts typically include those that recount a sequence of events, present past events as a narrative, discuss concepts and ideas, and argue a point of view.'

Exploration of sources, both primary and secondary, can include texts ranging from diaries and journals to historical literature and videos. Historical literature is a powerful tool for investigating historical concepts. The development of perspective in student writing can be based on engagement with and comparison of a range of texts about an historical event such as 'First contacts'. Suitable texts include:

Australians all by Nadia Wheatley and Ken Searle (2013)

The Rabbits by John Marsden and Shaun Tan (1998)

Nanberry: Black brother white by Jackie French (2011)

My place website (2011)

David Collin's Journal (1798)

Surgeon John White's Journal (1797)

Watkin Tench's Journal (1788)

'The First Fleet and first contact with local inhabitants' (Skwirk Online, 2005).

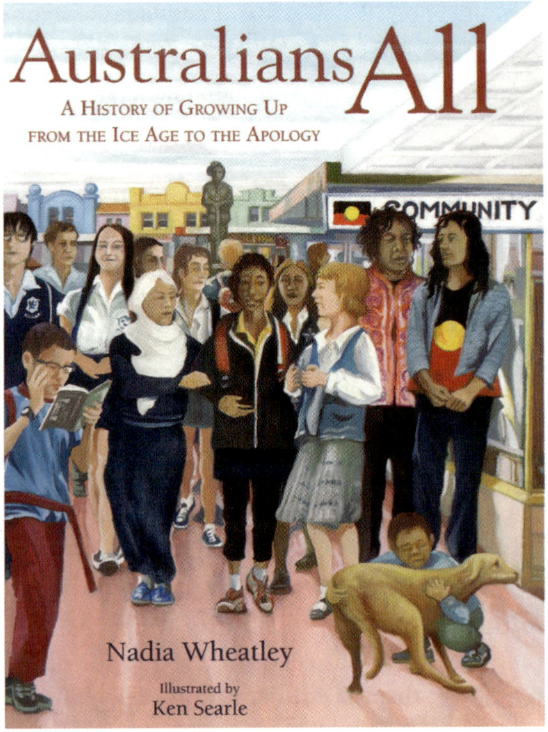

Figure 1
Cover of *Australians all*

In this example an extract from *Australians all* (Wheatley and Searle, 2013, p. 55) is placed against a range of other texts with a focus on how participants are named by writers in order to construct a particular perspective on historical events. The cover of the book is displayed in Figure 1.

Knowledge about texts and language

Choices for using the extract from *Australians all* (2013, p. 55) have been based on close analysis of its features and those of other texts based on similar events. This analysis in Table 1 reveals the possibilities for investigating perspective.

Table 1 Analysis of features of text conveying perspective

Context	*Australians all* by Nadia Wheatley and illustrated by Ken Searle, published in 2013, is a unique text in that it is a contemporary record of past events including the perspective of children in the form of mini-biographies. Wheatley (2013) points out that history books tend not to include the perspective of children. The accounts span from the time of the Ice Age to the Apology in 2008 and are based on historical research. When the selected text is placed beside other texts which record similar historical events it can be seen how history is problematic and influenced not only by the context of actual historical events but also by the context in which historical events are considered over the passing of time. By making particular language choices Nadia Wheatley attempts to capture the values, beliefs and perspectives surrounding historical events.
Social purpose/ genre	The social purpose of the text is complex. The text has narrative elements but merges historical events as well as persuasive elements to convey a particular interpretation of history. Texts can be categorised as imaginative, informative or persuasive. The primary purpose of this text is to inform, as it contains culturally important content thus being primarily informative. Such texts can include 'explanations and descriptions of natural phenomena, recounts of events, instructions and directions, rules and laws and news bulletins' (ACARA, 2012). Nadia Wheatley herself touches on the complexities of the purpose of the text in saying 'the reason I love history is because it is story' (2013, p. 253).

Field (What is the subject matter?)	The events in the chosen extract (Wheatley, 2013, p. 55) take place over a period of three days and are conveyed from the Indigenous perspective at the point of first contact with the British in 1788. The text is mainly action based with actions dominated by the British with the inclusion of some description. The participants in the text are clearly named from the perspective of the Indigenous community.
Tenor (Who is involved and what is the relationship?)	Based on the reader's world view and knowledge of past events, there may be different reactions to the text particularly in regards to how the British participants are described and named, eg, *the trespassers*. The reader is given a particular perspective of the events which often differs from other interpretations in both primary and secondary historical sources. The perspective is strengthened by the use of vocabulary to convey attitude, eg, *trespassers* (Humphrey, Droga & Feez, 2012) and the use of high modality, eg, *obviously*.
Mode (What is the channel of communication?)	In terms of the cohesive use of lexical items across the text, the reader needs to be able to track the participants by identifying the word chains (Derewianka, 2011) which serve to refer to the participants in a range of ways, eg, *more and more of the white devils, these aliens, one of the red coats.*
Text structure and phases	The text structure of the *Australians all* extract reflects a typical recount structure in which the reader is orientated to the situation in regards to the setting of time and place and introduced to the participants. In this case the naming of the participants provides the setting of the events, *the people of Botany Bay*. The next stage of the text is based on a sequence of events marked by reference to time, eg, *On the third morning.* Although the text is an extract, the concluding stage serves to provide a comment on the situation. The phases of the text reveal the recounting of events developed through problems with an attempted solution. In the final stage it is clear that the author is making a comment on the situation, a device often found in historical texts although not always obvious when embedded within events. (See annotated text in Table 2.)

Understanding features of a modelled text

The following analysis in Table 2 shows an extract from *Australians all* and the role of the noun group in naming participants in a variety of ways across the text. Often in the context of History the naming of participants reveals the perspective of the writer as an interpretation is conveyed about past events. Knowledge about such features assists students in critically analysing historical texts and also in composing their own texts. The following colour coding is used:

noun groups

Table 2 Analysis of text and language features

Text structure	Phases	*Australians all* by Nadia Wheatley and Ken Searle (2013, p. 55)
Orientation	Introduction of setting and participants	Over the next two days, the people of Botany Bay saw another ten ghost ships sail in from the horizon.
Sequence of events	Events/problems	They watched as more and more of the white devils began walking about on their homeland. Taking the water. Cutting the grass. Chopping down the trees
	Comment	These aliens obviously didn't have the slightest clue about the Law, or the right way to behave.
	Events/ attempted solution	Some of the men threw their spears, to let the trespassers know they were not welcome.
	Event	On the third morning, one of the redcoats made fire come out of a stick.
Comment	Comment on the overall situation	There was nothing to be done but wait patiently for the ghosts to go back into the clouds, as those other ones had done. Obviously they wouldn't stay here. This wasn't their country.

Focus on language for expressing ideas and interacting with others

Of significance in the extract from *Australians all* is the use of noun groups to name participants (human and non-human) across the text. Simultaneously they serve to name the participants involved in the actions whilst conveying a perspective about the nature of the participants. Comparison to other texts on similar events shows differences in such choices. When investigating the topic of 'first contact' the understanding of participants involved is critical to discussing perspectives and points of view.

By exploring the possibilities of the noun group we can start examining and questioning how participants are named in historical texts. Students can be given the potential elements of the noun group as a tool for looking at how to name, and as is often the case in History, how people are classified. This can be seen in these examples set out in Table 3.

Table 3 Noun groups naming participants across different texts						
Text	**Noun groups to name participants**					
	Pointer/ determiner	**Describer**	**Classifier**	**Main noun**	**Adjectival/ prepositional phrase**	**Adjectival clause**
Australians all (Wheatley, 2013)	the			people	of Botany Bay	
	these			aliens		
'The First Fleet and first contact with local inhabitants' (Skwirk, 2005)	the		Indigenous	communities		who tried to resist these strangers to their land
	the	new		settlers		

Refer to Derewianka (2011) and Humphrey, Droga & Feez (2012) for further explanation of the noun group.

The *Australian Curriculum: English* in Year 5 identifies the following content which can be addressed based on teacher preparation and knowledge about the chosen texts and language.

Language Understand that patterns of language interaction vary across social contexts and types of texts and that they help to signal social roles and relationships (ACELA1501)

Understand how noun groups/phrases and adjective groups/phrases can be expanded in a variety of ways to provide a fuller description of the person, place, thing or idea (ACELA1508)

Literature Use metalanguage to describe the effects of ideas, text structures and language features on particular audiences (ACELT1795)

Identify aspects of literary texts that convey details or information about particular social, cultural and historical contexts (ACELT1608)

Literacy Plan, draft and publish imaginative, informative and persuasive print and multimodal texts, choosing text structures, language features, images and sound appropriate to purpose and audience (ACELY1704)

Reread and edit student's own and others' work using agreed criteria for text structures and language features (ACELY1705)

Supporting the learner

Based on teacher knowledge about a range of texts and language choices, the following teaching and learning sequence (Figure 2) outlines steps to support students in moving from responding to a range of texts on an historical context to composing their texts to capture the perspective of an historical context.

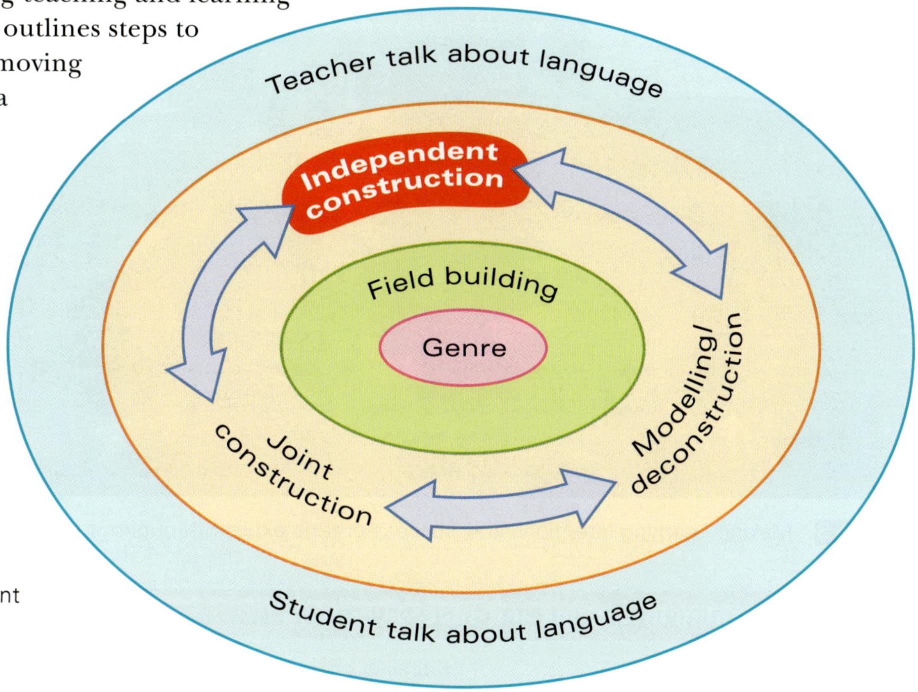

Figure 2
Adapted teaching and learning cycle with emphasis on independent construction

Spotlight on language for expressing ideas and interacting with others during independent writing

In this detailed example of independent construction, focus is placed on composing a text by drawing upon language developed throughout the teaching sequence, particularly through reading modelled texts. Through reading a range of texts students are equipped to make their language choices based on the historical context and the perspective they are wishing to convey to the reader.

Prior to writing discuss the 'Learning intentions and success criteria' set out in Table 4. This should be made familiar to students throughout the teaching cycle (See Figure 3). Sharing learning goals ensures students know what success looks like, making learning visible (Hattie, 2012) and also provides another avenue for sharing and developing metalanguage.

Figure 3 Making Learning intentions and Success criteria explicit throughout the whole teaching cycle

Table 4 Learning intentions and success criteria

Learning intentions	Success criteria
to understand how perspective is developed in historical texts	to identify how participants are named in texts to compare the naming of participants across a range of texts to use knowledge of naming participants in our own writing

To plan for independent writing, students can re-watch the *My place* video 'First contact'. Students should have already watched the video earlier in the teaching sequence. Figure 4 shows a still from the video.

Figure 4
My place video 'First contact Episode 24, 1788: *Dan*' (2011)

After viewing, students can record possible ways participants (Dan and Waruwi) may be named and described through noun group choice in order to show perspective (Table 5). By planning and revising earlier learning prior to writing, the table provides support even though students are writing independently.

Table 5 Naming participants to show perspective

Participants	Dan's perspective	Waruwi's perspective
'the British (Dan)'	Sir the Governor the men who don't know my secret ignorant men cheering marines	the ghosts the invaders the intruders the thieves who stole my dog
'the dog'	the friendly dog Lapa Waruwi's dog girl victim captive animal	Lapa my dog
'the Indigenous people (Waruwi)'	my new friend the honest native girl Waruwi who was frustrating my disappointed and betrayed friend	me my family nana

Students can then decide on whether to write in first or third person and from either Dan or Waruwi's perspective. This choice is significant when considering the writer's interaction with the reader (Derewianka, 2011) and can be discussed in terms of which choice might best convey the intended perspective to the reader. Students should also be reminded of the 'Learning intentions and Success criteria' (Table 4) before they begin writing.

After writing students can underline the noun groups which name participants and highlight choices which particularly convey perspective to the audience. Students may also evaluate themselves using a strategy such as 'three stars and a wish' in regards to the Learning intentions and

Success criteria. This involves identifying three positive aspects of their writing and a wish which identifies an area for improvement. Evaluation of choices supports self-assessment with the annotation of the text being key to leading to the development of self-knowledge, through feedback to self and peers (Hattie & Yates, 2014).

As can be seen in examples of student work below, as part of the teaching sequence students were given a pre-assessment task in which they recounted events from the video 'First contact'.

Figure 5
Sample of independent student writing (pre-assessment)

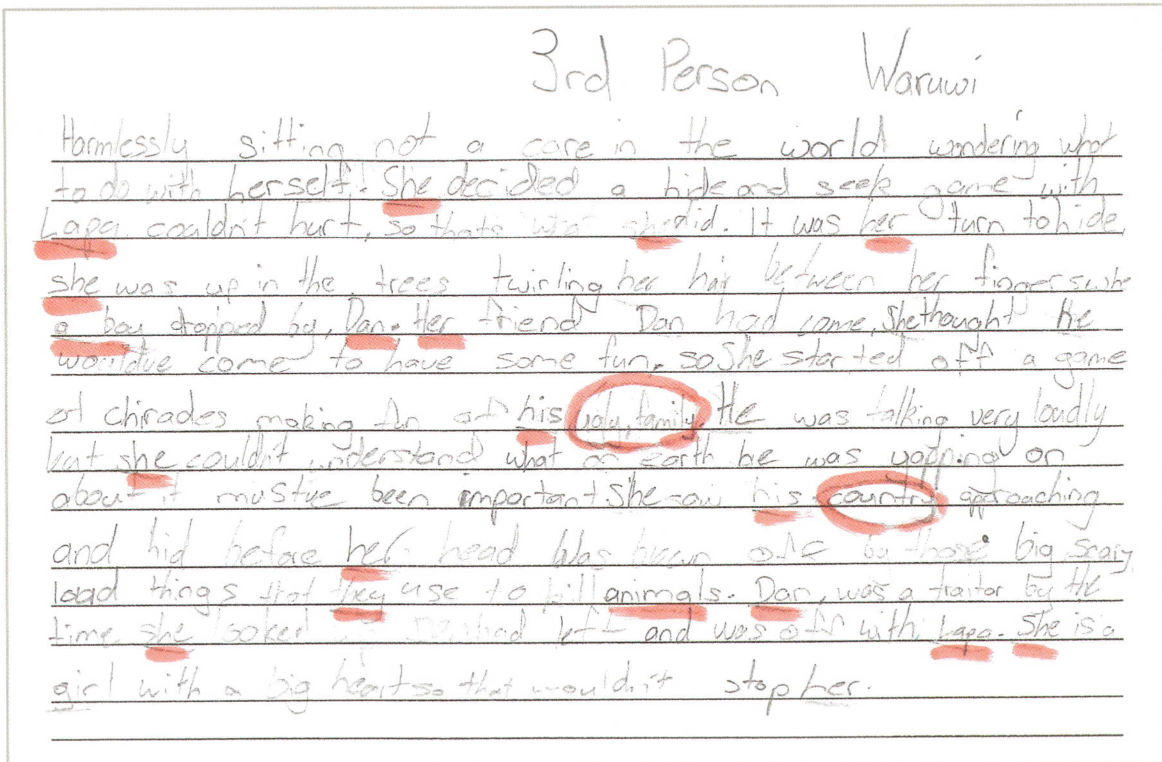

3rd Person Waruwi

Harmlessly sitting not a care in the world wondering what to do with herself! She decided a hide and seek game with Lapa couldn't hurt, so thats what she did. It was her turn to hide, she was up in the trees twirling her hair between her fingers when a boy stopped by, Dan. Her friend Dan had come, She thought he would've come to have some fun, so She started off a game of chirades making fun of his ugly family. He was talking very loudly but she couldn't understand what on earth he was yapping on about it must've been important. She saw his country approaching and hid before her head was blown off by those big scary loud things that they use to kill animals. Dan was a traitor by the time she looked Dan had left and was off with Lapa. She is a girl with a big heart so that wouldn't stop her.

In both the examples (Figures 5 and 6) the student chose to write in the third person from the perspective of Waruwi. As can be seen in the identification of noun groups to name the participants the post-assessment shows a more appropriate use of noun groups to convey perspective based on a more developed understanding of the historical context. In the first text (Figure 5) the emphasis is on the actions such as game playing and the sudden outcome of Dan being a traitor and taking Waruwi's dog.

By using more deliberate choices in naming Dan in particular, in the second text (Figure 6) the emphasis shifts to Waruwi's perception of

Dan through the way he is named which shifts to the broader context of participants invading her land through the use of noun groups built around nouns such as 'invaders' and 'intruders'.

In the second example, the choices move the events into an historical rather than personal retelling of events, serving to convey a particular perspective of the situation. Choices can be seen in Table 5.

Figure 6 Independent student writing (post-assessment)

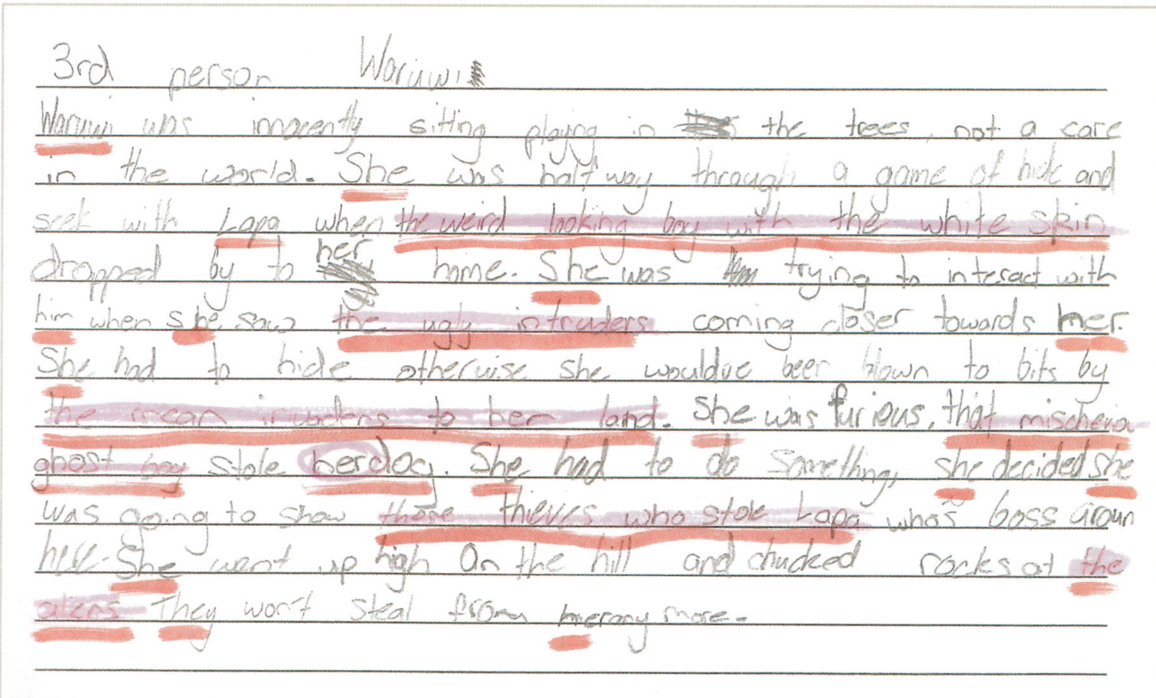

3rd person Waruwi

Waruwi was inocently sitting playing in the trees, not a care in the world. She was half way through a game of hide and seek with Lapa when the weird looking boy with the white skin dropped by to her home. She was trying to intesact with him when she saw the ugly intruders coming closer towards her. She had to hide otherwise she wouldve beer blown to bits by the mean intruders to her land. She was furious, that mischevious ghost boy stole her dog. She had to do something, she decided she was going to show those thieves who stole Lapa who's boss aroun here. She went up high on the hill and chucked rocks at the aliens. They won't steal from her any more.

Table 5 Comparison of language choices

Pre assessment		Post assessment	
Lapa	a boy	Waruwi	the weird looking boy with the white skin
a girl with a big heart	Dan, her friend	Lapa	the ugly intruders
	Dan		the mean intruders to her land
	his ugly family		that mischievous ghost boy
	his country		her dog
	a traitor		those thieves who stole Lapa
			the aliens

Summary of a teaching and learning sequence

Building the field

- Pre-assessment task to recount events from the *My place* website: 'First contact' (Figure 3).
- Introduce Learning intentions and Success criteria (Table 4).
- Questioning on how we learn about the past.
- Discuss sources of historical information (primary /secondary).
- Modelled reading to explore differing perspectives surrounding an historical event, eg 'My Country' by Dorothea Mackellar and 'Little Murri be a Murri before an Australian' by Lionel Fogarty. Compare different perspectives due to the writer's context. Conduct a Readers Theatre in which the two authors could meet and share their perspectives about an historical event.
- Use Floorstorming and 'I see, I think, I wonder' (Harvard Visible Thinking) to activate prior knowledge based on images of 'First contact'.

Text deconstruction/modelled reading

- Modelled reading of a range of texts, eg, *The Rabbits* (Marsden, J. & Tan S. 1998), *Australians all* (Wheatley, N. 2013), The 'First Fleet and first contact with local inhabitants' (Skwirk, 2005).
- Identify noun groups representing participants in a range of texts.
- Compare the meaning of the participants in conveying perspective across the texts.
- Small groups develop noun groups to name participants from images.
- View the *My place* video 'First contact Episode 24, 1788*: Dan'* (2011) which shows interaction between Dan, a British boy and an Aboriginal girl, Waruwi. Identify participants and perspectives.
- Continue linking learning to Learning intentions and Success criteria.

Joint construction

- Revisit Learning intentions and Success criteria.
- Re-watch the *My place* video: 'First Contact' and discuss participants.
- Name participants in a table to show varying perspectives of the situation (See Table 5).
- Play Conscience Alley (Drama Resource, 2014). This involves a group forming two lines facing each other. One student takes the role of Dan or Waruwi and walks between the lines. Those on one side give opposing advice to those on the other.
- Discuss choices for writing an historical recount and whether to use first or third person and from whose perspective it is to be written, ie Dan or Waruwi.
- Jointly construct a text with emphasis on participant choices through use of noun groups to convey perspective (see PETAA Paper 196 and video 'The critical conversation about text: Joint construction', Rossbridge & Rushton, 2014).

Independent construction

- Revisit Learning intentions and Success criteria.
- Re-watch *My place* video: 'First Contact'.
- Plan for writing by recording noun groups for naming and describing participants from a particular perspective.
- Students write a text to convey the perspective of one participant.
- After writing identify noun groups.
- Evaluate writing using 3 stars and a wish with reference to Learning intentions and Success criteria.

Resources

Australian Children's Television Foundation and Education Services Australia, 2011, *First contact*, viewed 24 October 2014, <http://www.myplace.edu.au/teaching_activities/1878_-_before_time/1788_1/1/first_contact_1788.html>.

Collins, D 1798, *An account of the English Colony of NSW Vol 1*, viewed 24 October 2014, < http://gutenberg.net.au/ebooks/e00010.html>

Fogarty, L 1995, *Little Murri Be a Murri before an Australian*, viewed 4 April 2015, <http://www.poetrylibrary.edu.au/poets/fogarty-lionel/little-murri-be-a-murri-before-an-australian-0214026>.

French, J 2011, *Nanberry: Black brother white*, Harper Collins, Sydney.

Mackellar, D 1908, *My country/Core of my heart*, viewed 4 April 2015, <http://www.sl.nsw.gov.au/discover_collections/natural_world/.../people_places/caergwrle/mycountry/index.html>.

Marsden, J & Tan, S 1998, *The Rabbits*, Lothian Books, Melbourne.

Rossbridge, J & Rushton, K. (2014) PETAA Paper 196 'The critical conversation about text: Joint construction', PETAA, Sydney. http://www.petaa.edu.au/teaching-resources/petaa-papers/PP-196

Skwirk Online, 2005 'The First Fleet and first contact with local inhabitants', viewed 24 October 2014, http://www.skwirk.com/p-c_s-17_u-455_t-1228_c-4698/first-contact-with-europeans/wa/first-contact-with-europeans/aboriginal-people-and-torres-strait-islanders/contact-with-europeans-the-effectsFirst Contact with Europeans>.

Tench, W 1788, *A narrative of the expedition to Botany Bay: with an account of New South Wales, its productions, inhabitants*, viewed 4 April 2015, <http://www.sl.nsw.gov.au/discover_collections/history_nation/terra_australis/published_accounts/tench/index.html >.

Wheatley, N & Searle, K. 2013, *Australians all: A History of growing up from the Ice Age to the Apology*, Allen and Unwin, Sydney.

White, J. 1790 *Journal of a Voyage to New South Wales*, viewed 24 October 2014,< http://gutenberg.net.au/ebooks03/0301531h.html >.

Drama Resource, viewed 23 March 2015, <http://dramaresource.com/strategies/conscience-alley>.

Harvard Visible Thinking Routines, viewed 23 March 2015, <http://www.visiblethinkingpz.org/VisibleThinking_html_files/03_ThinkingRoutines/03a_ThinkingRoutines.html>.

section three

Writing in the persuasive world

Writing persuasive texts can take place in a range of subject areas. The *Australian Curriculum: English* (2012) states that the primary purpose of persuasive texts is to 'put forward a point of view and persuade a reader, viewer or listener. They form a significant part of modern communication in both print and digital environments' (ACARA, 2012).

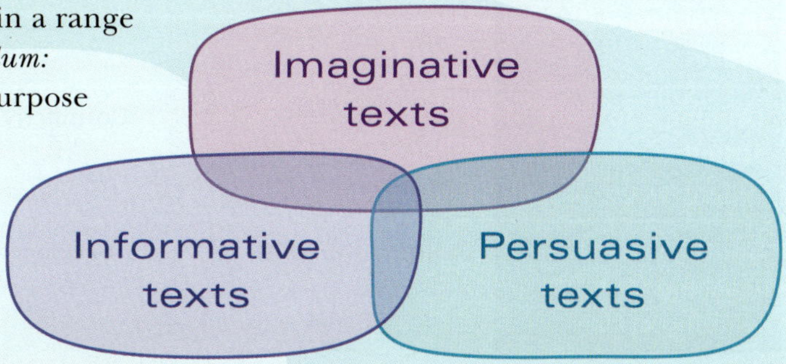

In this section, models of how to plan for and teach persuasive writing include:

- Model 1 Writing to evaluate behaviour (page 103)
- Model 2 Writing to persuade the community (page 114)
- Model 3 Writing to define a perspective (page 126)

When students are asked to compose persuasive texts, unlike imaginative or informative texts, the subject matter may concern either real or imagined worlds. Persuasive texts can include a range of texts such as expositions and discussions and even reviews and advertisements as in such texts arguments are presented to develop a perspective or point of view. Furthermore, 'It is worth noting that as students move through the school years and beyond, and find themselves using language to achieve increasingly complex purposes, the texts they produce are also more likely to exploit features of more than one type of text in innovative and creative ways.' (Humphrey, Droga & Feez, 2012, p. 161)

Section three			
Writing in the persuasive world			
Subject	English	Science	History
Writing	Discussion	Exposition	Exposition
Reading	*Parachute*	*School drop-off and pick-up zones*	'Stolen Child: Mathinna's story'
Language for expressing and connecting ideas		Connecting clauses and conjunctions	
Language for interacting with others	Evaluative vocabulary		
Language for text structure and organisation		Connectives	Nominalisation and passive voice
Spotlight on the teaching and learning cycle	Building the field	Text deconstruction	Independent writing

model one

Writing to evaluate behaviour

Writing	Discussion
Reading	*Parachute*
Language	Language for interacting: Evaluative vocabulary
Supporting the student	Building the field

This charming picture book, *Parachute* (Parker & Ottley, 2014), uses the metaphor of a parachute to reflect on the fears many young children experience. Toby is a boy who is afraid of heights and so he wears a parachute on his back every day until he overcomes his fear. Matt Ottley's whimsical images show Toby's cuddly toy tucked safely into the backpack parachute suggesting the usual object of comfort chosen by young children. In the story Toby never uses the parachute for himself, he only uses it once to save Henry, his cat. Furthermore when he does overcome his fear the pictures show Toby flying and climbing in a magical world, a clear indication that he does not need his parachute any more. This is a charming story with wonderful images and provides a safe place for young children to discuss their fears and how to overcome them.

Parachute is an example of how using a picture book in the English subject area can serve as stimulus and field building opportunity for writers of persuasive texts. The text provides a context for reflecting on fears and emotions, and further, can lead to discussion of perspectives through investigating evaluative language.

Figure 1
Parachute – Toby finally leaves his parachute aside

Knowledge about texts and language

This text provides many opportunities for a young reader to make connections to their own lives and by identifying with the emotions and fears of the character Toby provides support for a young author when trying to express opinions. The features of the chosen text are analysed in Table 1.

Table 1 Analysis of features of *Parachute*

Context	The author of this text, Danny Parker, is both a father and a teacher and according to the inside cover of this book, the illustrator, Matt Ottley, 'travels everywhere with a parachute, just in case...' Together these two men have created a text which is 'just right' for young children. It is both full of humour and fantasy but has within it layers which touch the real and commonly experienced childhood emotions.

Social Purpose/ genre	The social purpose of a traditional narrative is to entertain and instruct. This is a wonderful example of both, as the beautiful images and the simple text will allow young students to consider their own fears and imagine ways to combat them.
Field (What is the subject matter?)	The main theme is overcoming fear, in this case, the fear of falling. Toby uses his parachute as a way of keeping his fears at bay but in actual fact his parachute would be of no use in most of the situations encountered in the text. When this is acknowledged it can be seen that Toby is comforting himself with the parachute rather than taking realistic steps to prevent a fall. However in the end it is his action of saving his cat and then the self-talk which accompanies that act that helps him to overcome his fear.
Tenor (Who is involved and what is the relationship?)	While the question of 'who tells' can only be relevant for verbal text, that of 'who sees' is pertinent for both verbal and visual strands of meaning. The viewer can be positioned to assume different viewing personas. The viewer can be an outside observer or alternatively be someone 'participating' fleetingly in that world through a relationship with, or identification as, one of the characters (Painter, Martin & Unsworth, 2013, p. 18). Focalisation, or point of view relates to who is narrating. In this case it is in the third person, but at some points in the text the action is seen from the character's point of view. This is especially clear in the exaggeration of height of the stool or tree, the images which accompany this verbal text: *for getting out of bed in the morning, for when he finished his breakfast, and after he brushed his teeth.*
Mode (What is the channel of communication?)	The channel of communication is written but the writing is very spoken-like as it is aimed at young children who will readily participate with this text. The images are also carrying much of the story as they work in combination with the verbal text.
Text structure and phases	The structure and phases are typical of a story genre as the reader is orientated through the introduction of the character and setting. A series of events is developed to demonstrate situations in which the character feels unsafe. The problem is solved as the character confronts his fears.

Understanding features of a modelled text

Examples of the verb groups or processes have been indentified in Table 2. These have been identified as they indicate the character's behaviour. The following colour coding has been used for this purpose:

verb groups/processes

Words indicating judgement of behaviour are in bold.

Table 2 Analysis of text and language features

Text structure/ stage	Phase	*Parachute*
Orientation	Setting	Toby always wore a parachute.
	Comment	It was most useful
Series of events	(This list of situations in which Toby feels unsafe can be used to show the reason he is afraid, eg. he is afraid he might fall.)	for getting out of bed in the morning, for when he finished his breakfast and after he brushed his teeth. His parachute made him feel **safe** on the swings ^ and the see-saw ^ and the slide. Or whenever **danger** might strike
	(Note Toby's fears by examining the verbal and visual text as the angle in many of the images exaggerates the height of the stool or tree and indicates Toby was afraid of heights as he felt small and vulnerable.)	The tree house was high. And Henry was even higher. The ladder swung as Toby clambered up.
Complication		He didn't look **down**. "Come on Henry!" called Toby as he reached the branch. "Don't be scared," said Toby as he put out his hand.
Resolution		Little by little Henry floated to the ground. And was **safe**.
	Comment	Suddenly, Toby was **alone**. "Come on Toby!" he said to himself.

	Effect	**"There's nothing to fear"**
	Problem	he said
	Reaction	as he held on **tight**.
	(The text is repeating what Toby did and said when he saved his cat Henry, but now his words and thoughts are for himself.)	."Just try to keep **calm**."
Coda	Solution	Little by little step by step ... Toby climbed down.
	Comment	And was safe.
	(The metaphor is continued here to indicate that Toby had found a way of overcoming his fears by acting and reflecting on his actions)	As time passed, Toby needed his parachute less and less. And one day, he left it behind.

Focus on language for expressing and interacting with others

In *Parachute* the reader is required to make inferences about the character's behaviour as it changes through the text. This is conveyed by both the written and visual text and is achieved primarily through the use of verb groups or processes chosen in the stages of the text. The words that indicate judgement of Toby's behaviour are bolded in the modelled text (Humphrey, Droga & Feez, 2012, p. 102). These words have a function of telling us about the experience but simultaneously encourage the reader to evaluate Toby's behaviour thus also having an interpersonal function.

The *Australian Curriculum: English* identifies the following content in Year 2 which can be addressed based on teacher preparation and knowledge about texts and language.

Language	Understand that different types of texts have identifiable text structures and language features that help the text serve its purpose (ACELA1463)
	Identify language that can be used for appreciating texts and the qualities of people and things (ACELA1462)

Literature	Compare opinions about characters, events and settings in and between texts (ACELT1589)
Literacy	Create short imaginative, informative and persuasive texts using growing knowledge of text structures and language features for familiar and some less familiar audiences, selecting print and multimodal elements appropriate to the audience and purpose (ACELY1671)

Supporting the learner

Based on teacher knowledge about the features of *Parachute* the following teaching and learning sequence looks at how to use literature to build the field in preparation for writing a discussion (Figure 2). A focus on evaluative language is developed through engaging with the narrative genre and this knowledge about language can then be applied to the discussion genre as students discuss emotions.

Figure 2
Adapted teaching and learning cycle with emphasis on field building

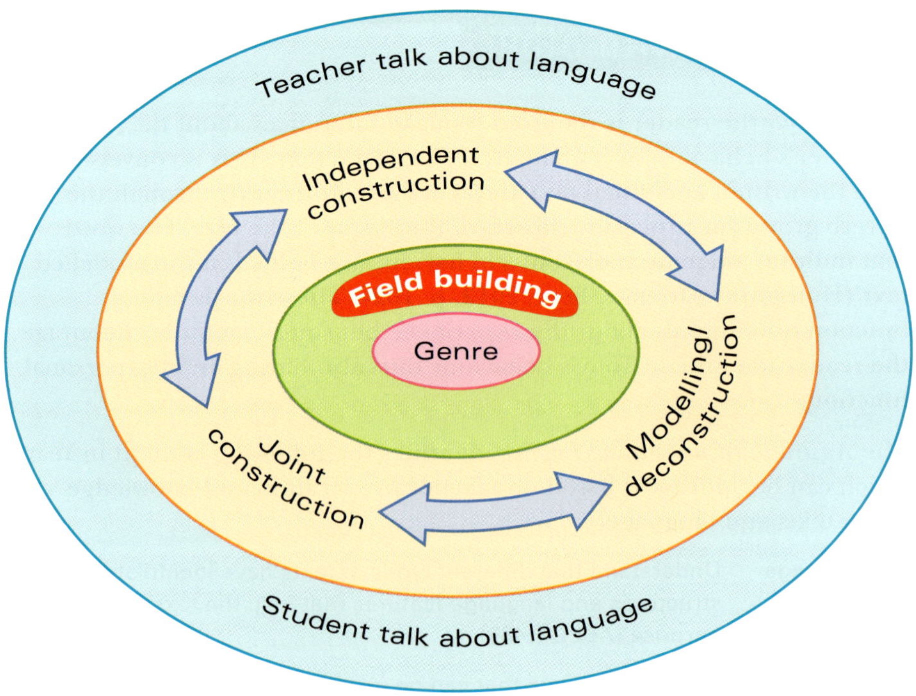

Spotlight on language for interacting with others during field building for a discussion

Following a modelled reading of *Parachute* develop a cline to support students' use of evaluative vocabulary and judgement about Toby and his behaviour. Figure 3 from the text shows Toby saving his cat, Henry, by using his parachute. At this point in the text the reader already knows about the fears Toby experiences, so this is a great moment to judge his behaviour using words from the text. Provide some words that could possibly describe the worst of Toby's behaviour, *weird, odd,* because he wears a parachute everywhere and *cowardly* because he is so frightened of heights and of falling. Offer more words that describe the best of his personality such as *normal, brave, capable,* as these can be seen in both the visual and verbal text as he attempts to save his cat. Design a cline

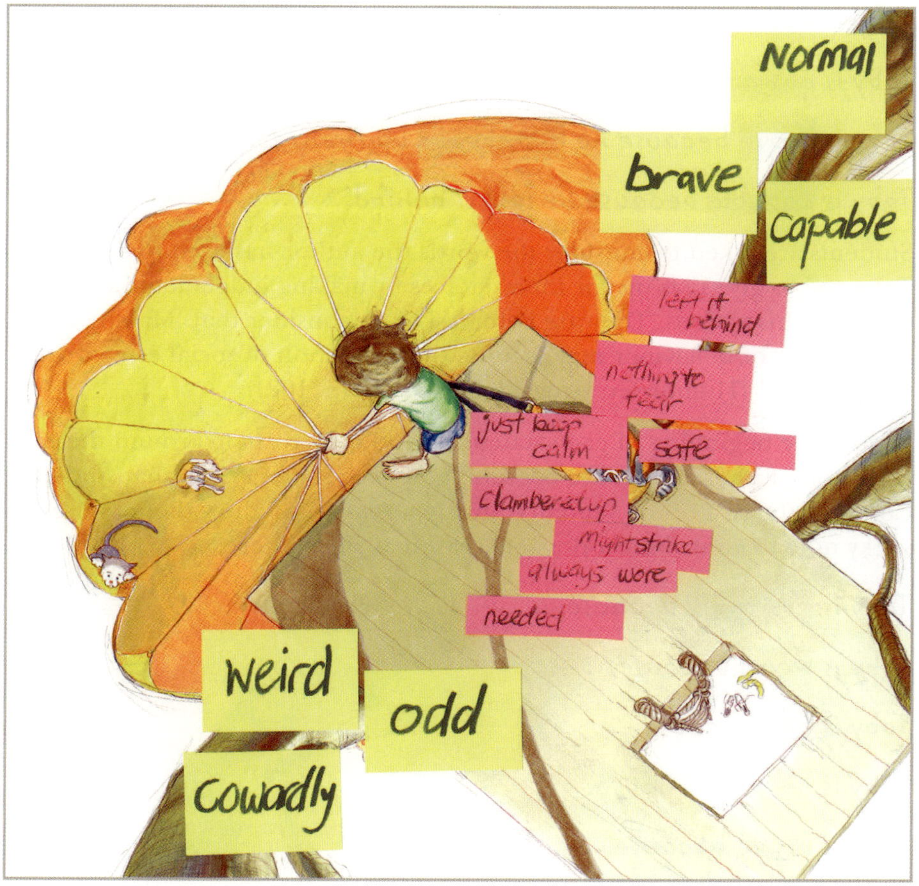

Figure 3
Students place words from the text and synonyms on a cline to show Toby's transition from frightened to brave as he uses his parachute to save his cat.

by providing an enlarged copy of an image from the text which shows a branch of the tree Toby is climbing. Support students to use sticky notes to place words along this cline to show Toby's transition from fearful to brave. Drawing from the text and using the branch of the tree in this image, which provides a diagonal line, select words or phrases that show Toby's transition (Figure 3). Moving from the bottom to the top of the cline, some of the words might be: *needed*; *always wore*; *might strike*; *clambered up*; *just keep calm*; *safe*; *nothing to fear*; *left it behind*. The words that indicate judgement of Toby's behaviour are bolded in the modelled text (Humphrey, Droga & Feez, 2012, p. 102).

As students select words from the text suggest that they give a reason for their judgement using the words that have been supplied such as: *normal, brave, capable and weird, odd, cowardly*. In the text below the adjectives showing judgement are highlighted in purple and the verbs/processes are in green.

Toby is odd because he always wore a parachute.

Toby is cowardly because he always thinks danger might strike.

Toby is brave because he clambered up the tree.

Toby is capable because he left it behind.

Students are asked to consider the words the author has used to describe Toby and to give reasons for their choices by making judgements about him from his actions. They are being asked to consider that 'Making moral judgements of behaviour may include the evaluation of social esteem and competence' (Humphrey, Droga & Feez, 2012, p. 102).

Record the beginning of each statement and display them around the classroom. Either record the beginning of each statement so that students can write the rest of the sentence, giving a reason, or allow them to use a sticky note to contribute a possible reason as shown here.

Toby is cowardly because...

Toby is weird because...

Toby is odd because...

Toby is normal because...

Toby is brave because...

OR

Because he ______________________________ Toby is capable.

What did he do? What did he say?

Encourage students to use the text to find reasons as in the preceding oral language activity.

Many aspects of developing a written discussion are shared with the preparation necessary for a debate. Many public speaking and debating strategies are very useful for field building in preparation for writing a discussion. The following activities have all been adapted from 'Taking the initiative' (Cameron & Davey, 2012) and focus on the use of oral language in developing thinking.

- After students discuss their views of Toby, ask one student to role-play a judge. Tell the judge that it has been decided that Toby is cowardly, weird and odd but that everyone in the room thinks there has been a mistake and have formed a protest group called 'Friends of Toby'. Allow students to volunteer to plead for a change of judgement about Toby using the evidence the class has gathered. After all those who wish to speak have made their pleas for Toby, ask the judge to sum up the evidence and make a judgement.
- Play Verbal ping pong. When students are familiar with the idea that a person's behaviour can be evaluated and a judgement can be made and supported by reasons, the idea of presenting opposing views in a discussion can be developed. Point out to students that in a discussion although both points of view are presented, like the judge in the role-play, eventually one point of view is chosen and a recommendation is made. Divide the class into two groups and assign them to a side, either affirmative or negative, for the topic, 'Toby is a hero'. Draw up two columns and encourage each team to present a point to support their perspective. Record the points and reward each group for their point but provide an extra reward for any point that rebuts a point made by the opposing team. For instance: 'Toby is not a hero because he was afraid.' Rebutted by: 'Toby is a hero because even though he was afraid, he saved his cat.'

Spending time in developing ideas about the purpose, structure and language used in a discussion will result in students who quickly engage in writing a jointly constructed text as they will have developed understandings from word to text level relating to the topic. Figure 4 is one such sample of joint construction. Using a range of texts in which the main character acts in spite of their fears will further help students to develop their understandings about how to take and support a perspective using evaluative vocabulary suitable for the context (shown in purple).

Figure 4

Joint construction sample where students use evaluative vocabulary developed from the text to discuss an issue.

> **Children should be brave.**
>
> I think that we should be brave because firstly it could help to keep us safe. Secondly we could have more fun. Also we could do more things if we weren't afraid. Children can get a head start on learning to be brave so when they're an adult they will definitely survive.
>
> It is dangerous to do things without thinking about them first and it is not cowardly to be afraid. It is normal to be afraid but we have to think about our feelings and decide if this is a good time to be brave or if there's nothing to fear.
>
> All in all children should be brave because they will get to try new things and have more fun.

Summary of a teaching and learning sequence

Field building

- Read *Parachute* and develop a cline to support students' use of evaluative vocabulary and judgement.
- Develop understanding of evaluative vocabulary through oral language games.

Text deconstruction

- During modelled reading, students sort and classify evaluative words on a cline and identify words from *Parachute* that evaluate the character's attributes.
- Show examples of discussion texts and how these compare with narrative texts.
- Identify evaluative language used in both narrative and discussion texts.

Joint construction

- Jointly construct a discussion and encourage students to use evaluative vocabulary developed through the teaching and learning cycle.

Independent construction

- In pairs or small groups students independently write a discussion on one of the topics developed when undertaking the field building activities.

Resources

Cameron, L. & Davey, T. 2012, 'Taking the initiative NSW Department of Education and Communities' <https://www.artsunit.nsw.edu.au/sites/default/files/Taking_the_Initiative.pdf>.

Parker, D & Ottley, M 2014, *Parachute,* LittleHare Books, Richmond, Vic.

model two

Writing to persuade the community

Writing	Exposition
Reading	*School drop-off and pick-up zones*
Language	Language for connecting ideas, text structure and organisation: clause combinations, conjunctions and connectives
Supporting the student	Text deconstruction

This teaching and learning sequence was developed through the integration of the English, Science and Personal Development subject areas. With particular focus on Science as a Human Endeavour and investigation of how 'science knowledge helps people to understand the effect of their actions' (ACARA, Year 3, 2012). Persuasive texts can be developed on a range of topics. In this example, students look at ways to communicate with the school community to persuade them to act in a certain way. When writing students can take a position on limiting the use of cars for short trips, such as driving students to school, due to the impact on the local environment.

As part of field building and showing the role of science in our everyday lives a number of walk and ride-to-school campaigns can be investigated. There are several websites with useful information on the subject for students' reference and are provided in the Resources section of this model.

The websites show how persuasive texts are composed by organisations in order to encourage behavioural changes in communities. Through reading a range of information on various sites, students can collect key information relating to science and in particular to the relationship between human activity and the environment. This places a focus on developing knowledge about areas such as vehicle emissions, greenhouse gases and noise pollution, while information on issues such as safety and health also arise.

The modelled text is based on the topic of 'School drop-off and pick-up zones'. This text has been selected to model the genre through a topic on which students may have some background knowledge. Once students have learnt about the features of the genre they can then move into preparing for writing to parents about no longer driving cars to school because of the need to protect the environment. The genre and audience remains the same and the field is similar but varies enough to move the writing into the more scientific field.

Knowledge about texts and language

The choices for using *School drop-off and pick-up zones* as a modelled text have been based on close analysis of its features (Table 1), and to show how these assist in connecting ideas within the text in relation to the staging and purpose of the text.

Table 1 Analysis of features of *School drop-off and pick-up zones*

Context	*School drop-off and pick-up zones* has been developed from a template provided by a government road safety organisation (Centre for Road safety, NSW Government) in which institutions such as schools are encouraged to communicate with the broader community to promote road safety. This is common in Western democracies where initiatives are developed and often funded for the greater good of communities. The social context for publishing such a text can be in the school newsletter be it on paper or electronic.
Social purpose/ genre	The social purpose of the text is to persuade the parent community, who is the target audience, to respond with a particular action, that is, to support the new school drop-off and pick-up zone for students. In the form of a letter, this is an example of the hortatory (urging or encouraging) exposition genre as the writer is trying to persuade the reader to behave in a certain way (see Humphrey, Droga & Feez, 2012).

Field (What is the subject matter?)	The subject matter of the text evolves around the notion of a school drop-off and pick-up zone with the major participants being the school community, including both parents and students. As well, it touches on concepts such as initiative, system and safety. Combinations of clauses create different relationships between the ideas being expressed and connected. As a result, connections between ideas are created through combinations of independent and dependent clauses, often with the use of conjunctions.
Tenor (Who is involved and what is the relationship?)	The text is an example of how, as audiences become less familiar to the writer when writing to persuade, a shift occurs from stating personal opinions to more impersonal and objective expression of subject matter. Evaluation is conveyed particularly in regards to social value, as vocabulary such as *faster, less busy, safer* is used in the text to convey the worth of participating in the new initiative.
Mode (What is the channel of communication?)	The mode of the text is written with a logical structure supporting development of arguments and creating coherence through choices at text level. In this text, connectives such as *in addition* and *therefore* have been used to add arguments and make conclusions.
Text structure and phases	A predictable text structure is used. Firstly it addresses the audience and then introduces the topic with a position statement. This is followed by arguments and finally a reiteration of the appeal. The phases are also quite predictable as background is added to the issue in the position statement and the arguments are developed logically through points and elaboration (refer to Derewianka & Jones, 2012). See Table 2 for the analysis of the text and structure.

Understanding features of a modelled text

Through analysis of the *School drop-off and pick-up zones* in Table 2, the text and language features that will assist in determining a focus for developing a teaching sequence have been identified. In this case the analysis focuses on the connecting of ideas across the stages of the text. The following colour coding and symbols have been used in this analysis:

verb groups/processes

independent clause   dependent clause

end of a clause //
end of a clause at the end of a sentence ///

conjunctions   connectives

Table 2 Analysis of text and language features

Text structure	Phases	*School drop-off and pick-up zones* (adapted from http://roadsafety.transport.nsw.gov.au/downloads/dropoffpickup/dropoffpickup_organise_dl1.html)
Address		Dear Parent/Carer,
Statement of position	Issue and background information	A new school 'Drop-off and Pick-up' student marshalling initiative will be commencing at our school soon. /// (simple sentence)
		Under this system, a driver pulls in to a designated *No Parking* zone //
		and a supervising adult volunteer assists the students //
		to exit or enter the vehicle from the kerbside doors only. /// (complex sentence)
	Appeal	We encourage all parents in the school community //
		to take part in this initiative //
		as it will result in many safety advantages for our students. /// (complex sentence)
Arguments	Point	Most importantly, the 'Drop off and Pick Up' zone will relieve traffic congestion around the school. /// (simple sentence)
	Elaboration	Parents won't need to park a long way from the school //
		or wait for long periods of time in the *No Parking* zone. /// (compound sentence)
		Therefore school pick up and drop off times should be faster and less busy. /// (simple sentence)
	Point	In addition, students will be safer //
		when arriving //
		and leaving the school grounds. // (complex sentence)
	Elaboration	There will be more adult supervision //
		as students are being dropped off //
		and picked up from the school. /// (complex sentence)
		As a result students will feel safer with increased supervision //
		because the community will be taking greater responsibility for student safety. /// (complex sentence)

Reiteration of appeal	Appeal and directions	Full community support for this initiative is encouraged. /// (simple sentence) To participate // please call into the office // and pick up further information. /// (complex sentence)

Focus on language for connecting ideas, text structure and organisation

Related to the field of a text is the linking of ideas in clauses to show relationships. As students move through schooling, texts become more complex. Particularly in the case of persuasive texts, the relationship between chunks of meaning or clauses results in different types of sentence choices. These choices depend on what the writer is trying to convey to the audience. In the modelled text a variety of clause/sentence choices have been used as the writer moves through the stages of the text and develops the arguments by promoting the beneficial results of taking part in the school drop-off and pick-up zone.

Knowing about sentence and clause types in isolation is not particularly useful unless the connections between clauses are considered in relation to the purpose of the text. As students move through schooling, talk about clause and sentence types for considering the connection of ideas and text organisation will become more explicit. However it is important for teachers to have sufficiently in-depth knowledge about the texts that are being modelled and composed in order to make choices as to the kinds of conversations with students that can be developed.

Figure 1
Sentence types

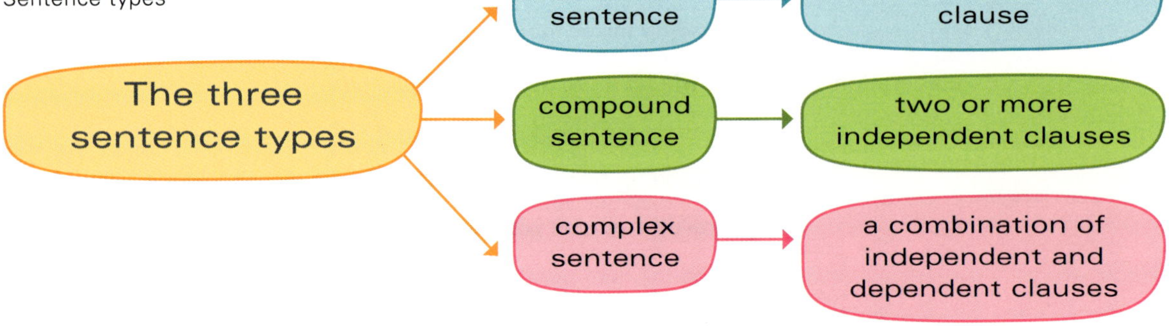

When discussing sentence types with students an assumption is made that they are aware of clauses and their types. The knowledge of clauses is necessary, as a simple sentence is not necessarily a short sentence just as a complex sentence is not necessarily a lengthy sentence. The sentence type is determined by the combination of clauses as shown in Figure 1. (See Derewianka, 2011 and Humphrey, Droga & Feez, 2012).

As is evident in the modelled text, an independent clause can stand alone, while a dependent clause adds additional circumstantial information to an independent clause. The independent clause is a little like the truck that pulls the trailer which is the dependent clause (Figure 2).

Figure 2
The independent and dependent clause

Often clauses are connected through the use of conjunctions. The conjunctions may be coordinating (eg, *and, but, so, or, neither, nor, yet*) as they join two independent clauses together. Conjunctions can also be subordinate as they can join dependent and independent clauses (See examples from the modelled text in Table 2). The choice of conjunction is determined by the relationship the writer wishes to express between the ideas.

Another way of adding detail is the use of a particular type of dependent clause known as a non-finite clause. A non-finite clause is a 'stripped back' clause, usually without an explicit subject, modality, tense or subordinating conjunction (Derewianka, 2011, p. 98). For example, 'to take part in this initiative'.

In addition to relationships established through clause type and conjunction choices, connections can also be made at a text level through the use of connectives. This relates to the mode of the text as their use supports the overall structure of the text. In a persuasive text we would typically expect to see connectives used to add and sequence arguments and also show cause or result (see Table 2). To distinguish between conjunctions and connectives their function needs to be considered. The role of conjunctions is to make connections between ideas or clauses while connectives make logical connections across sentences and paragraphs thus providing overall text cohesion.

The *Australian Curriculum: English* identifies the following content in Year 3 which can be addressed based on teacher preparation and knowledge about texts and language.

Language	Understand how different types of texts vary in use of language choices, depending on their purpose and context (for example, tense and types of sentences) (ACELA1478)
Literacy	Plan, draft and publish imaginative, informative and persuasive texts demonstrating increasing control over text structures and language features and selecting print, and multimodal elements appropriate to the audience and purpose (ACELY1682)

Supporting the learner

In the detailed example that follows, text deconstruction is the focus for drawing explicit attention to 'using appropriate simple, compound and complex sentences to express and combine ideas' and 'selecting appropriate text structure for a writing purpose and sequencing content for clarity and audience impact' (ACARA, Year 3, ACELY1682). By the early primary years, students should have an understanding of clauses. A starting point for talking about clauses and sentence types may be to look at the function of conjunctions and connectives in the modelled text.

Figure 3
Adapted teaching and learning cycle with emphasis on text deconstruction

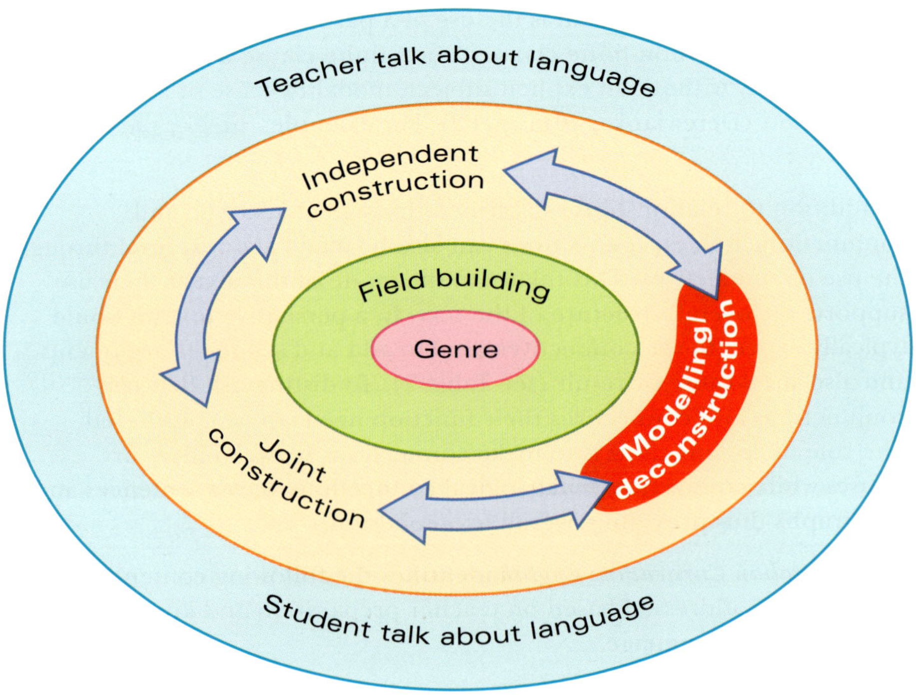

Spotlight on language for connecting ideas, text structure and organisation during text deconstruction

Prior to deconstructing the text (Figure 3), the purpose and audience of the text should be discussed and the stages and phases of the text identified. The modelled text can be unpacked to show the use of conjunctions as well as connectives across the text with guided discussion about how they relate to the text structure and phases of a persuasive text.

When looking at a sample text deconstruction (Figure 4) it becomes apparent that coordinating conjunctions are often used to add information while subordinating conjunctions (eg, *when, as, because*) are particularly associated with linking ideas through time and reason. These serve to connect main ideas related to the issue with elaborating points which help develop the arguments. In addition the connectives (eg, *therefore, as a result, in addition*) are playing a slightly different role in that they are making connections across the text by summing up the results of actions or adding additional arguments. Students can be encouraged to link and identify the function of the conjunctions and connectives to the stages of the text and ultimately to the purpose.

Figure 4
Deconstruction of the modelled text

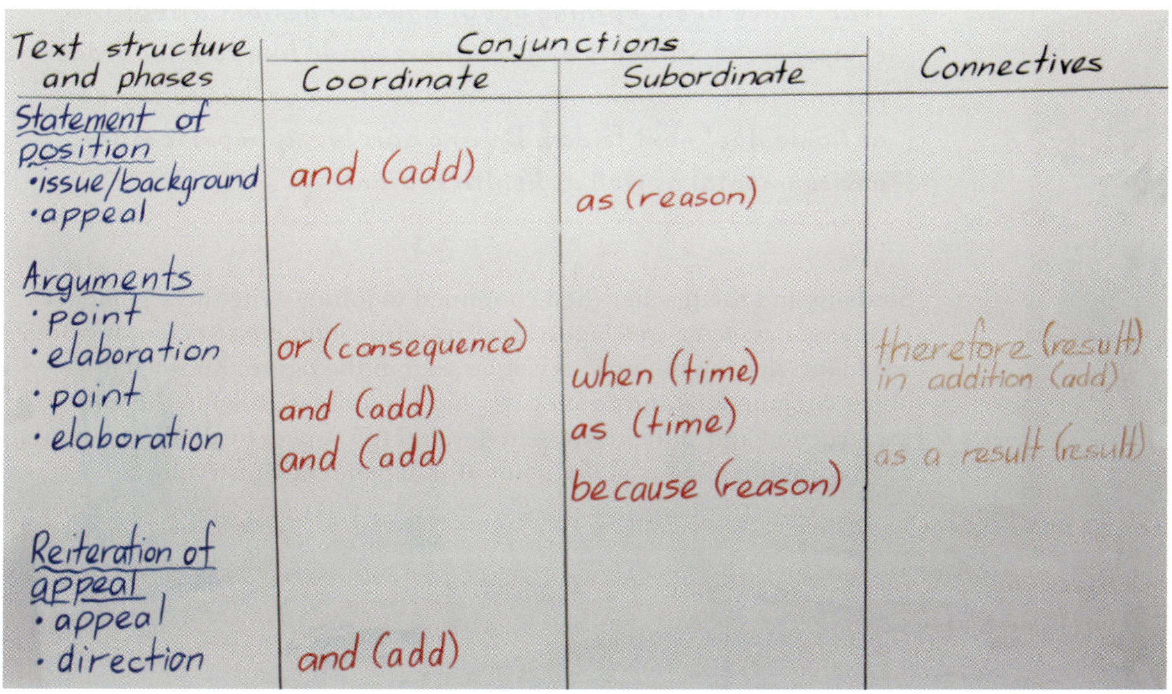

Text structure and phases	Conjunctions: Coordinate	Conjunctions: Subordinate	Connectives
Statement of position • issue/background • appeal	and (add)	as (reason)	
Arguments • point • elaboration • point • elaboration	or (consequence) and (add) and (add)	when (time) as (time) because (reason)	therefore (result) in addition (add) as a result (result)
Reiteration of appeal • appeal • direction	and (add)		

As stated before, this can be a starting point before students move into talking about clause and sentence types and their function within the text. This should progress across the years of schooling. When looking at the dependent clauses it can be seen that the subordinate conjunctions or the non-finite clauses often add results and reasons or information about time. These choices are critical to the arguments being presented to the reader about why they should be involved in the drop-off and pick-up zone. Conversation can start with talking about the clauses that stand on their own and express the issue and argument, as opposed to the clauses that do not stand on their own as they elaborate or add detail to the main ideas or arguments.

In the sample of student writing following, they used their knowledge from the text deconstruction to participate in a joint construction of a letter to persuade parents to take part in a 'Leave the car at home day'. The arguments were based on the environmental effects of driving cars short distances.

On one day the students jointly constructed the following statement of position.

> Dear Parents,
>
> Year 3 have been learning about how our actions affect the environment. Students and teachers would like to encourage parents in the community to take part in our 'Leave the car at home day' next Friday. Driving cars less is important for environmental as well as health reasons.

Students and the teacher then continued to jointly write the arguments a couple of days later (see Figure 5). Part of the joint construction involved a student 'sharing the pen' as can be seen in the figure. Knowledge about conjunctions and connectives has been highlighted in the joint construction and students were to develop this aspect further when editing and redrafting in pairs at the point of independent construction.

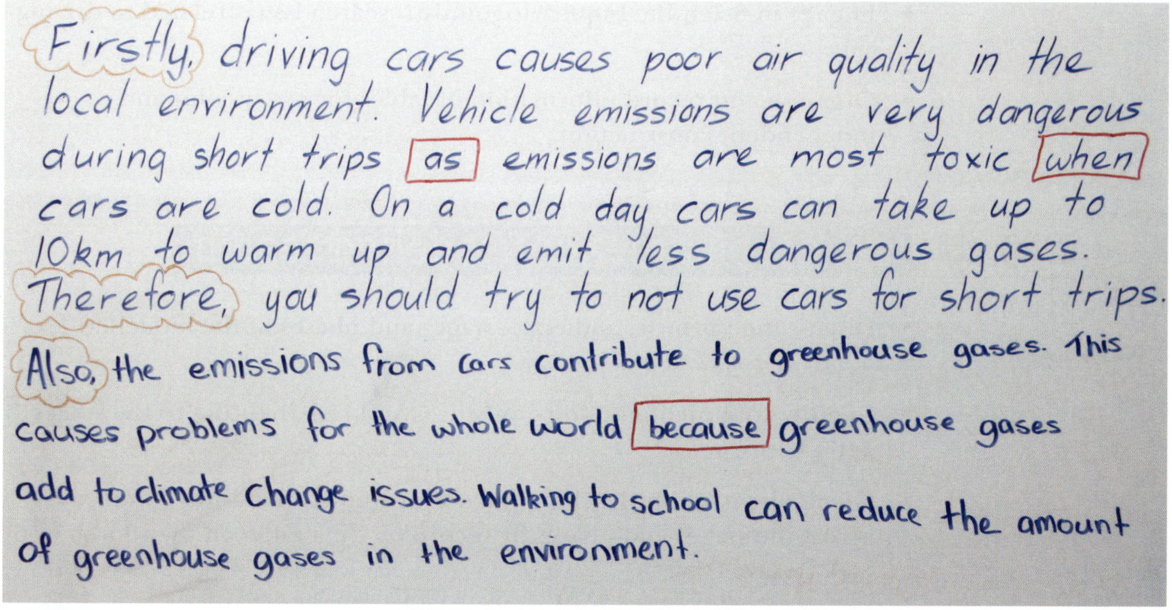

Figure 5 A sample of joint construction

Summary of a teaching and learning sequence

Building the field

- Explore campaigns such as *Walk safely to school day* and *Diabetes Australia Walk to Work Day* to locate issues on the effects on the environment of choices people make.
- Compare the purpose of the range of texts on the websites of the campaigns and discuss the subject matter and target audiences.
- Locate templates for promoting campaigns to the community and discuss the context and audience and how this might apply to their own school context.

- Engage in Scientific Inquiry to jointly research issues related to driving cars.
- Organise and record information in tables for use in joint and independent construction.

Text deconstruction/modelled reading

- Discuss the purpose, audience, stages and phases of the modelled text *School drop-off and pick-up zones.*
- Identify conjunctions and connectives and link their use to the stages and phases.
- Guide discussion by tracking the use of conjunctions and connectives across the stages and phases by recording on a table on the whiteboard (see Figure 4).
- Discuss clause/sentence choices and their function in elaborating or adding detail across the text.

Joint construction

- Develop a school-based campaign for *Leave the car at home day.* Discuss who in the community would need to be informed and the relationship between the students as writers and their audience, i.e. parents.
- Provide a template (eg. Walk Safely to School Day newsletter insert http://www.walk.com.au/WSTSD/images/elements/contentpics/2015/NewsletterInsert_2015.pdf) and use as the basis for jointly constructing a letter to parents to be placed in the school newsletter.
- Identify arguments in the researched information that would assist parents in being persuaded to change their behaviour.
- Jointly write a letter to parents with reference to researched information in tables and paying attention to connecting ideas through clause choices and use of conjunctions and connectives. During the process 'share the pen' with students.

Independent construction

- In pairs, using the jointly constructed text, students identify the use of conjunctions/connectives and sentence types and check that a range are used across the text in order to develop arguments and in particular elaborate on key points.
- Students redraft the texts and explain changes through talking about how connections were made between ideas and how this assisted in making the text persuasive and appropriate for the audience.

Resources

Kidsed.com, viewed 5 April, <http://yourkidsed.com.au/info/four-great-reasons-why-kids-should-walk-to-school >.

Walk Safely to School Day, viewed 5 April, <http://www.walk.com.au/WSTSD/how-to-participate.asp >.

Walk Safely to School Day newsletter insert, viewed 5 April, <http://www.walk.com.au/WSTSD/images/elements/contentpics/2015/NewsletterInsert_2015.pdf >.

Diabetes Australia Walk to Work Day, viewed 5 April, <http://www.walk.com.au/wtw/Page.asp?PageID=1264>.

WalkBike to school, viewed 5 April,<http://www.walkbiketoschool.org/ready/why-walk-or-bike/cleaner-environment >.

NSW Government, Centre for Road safety, 'Drop off and pick up initiative, parent letter', viewed 5 April, <http://roadsafety.transport.nsw.gov.au/downloads/dropoffpickup/dropoffpickup_organise_dl1.html)>

model three

Writing to define a perspective

Writing	Exposition
Reading	'Stolen Child: Mathinna's story'
Language	Language for creating cohesive texts: passive voice and nominalisation
Supporting the student	Independent writing

This teaching and learning sequence was developed in the History subject area with several aims. One is to support students to engage in the history of Australia and, in this case, to develop an understanding of the relationships that were developed with Aboriginal people in the earliest years by understanding that settlement was also invasion. It addresses this important subject matter but also spends time looking at the language resources that allow an author to present a perspective or argue a point of view, both important aspects of the historian's work.

Reading an informative text to gain information about the subject matter before writing is common practice in primary schools. However in subject areas other than English it is almost always the case that the text selected for modelled reading will be informative and may not be in the same genre as the written text students will be asked to compose. It is therefore important to select a text which has at least some relevant features that can be discussed. As in this case, the structure, audience and purpose are different because the modelled text recounts a life and the written text is persuasive. The subject matter in the modelled text is Mathinna, an Aboriginal girl from Tasmania who was taken away from her family as a result of the frontier wars.

This portrait of Mathinna (Figure 1) was commissioned by Lady Franklin and painted by Thomas Bock in 1842. It now hangs in the Tasmanian Museum and Art Gallery in Hobart. In the teacher's guide to the exhibition, on page 8, it states:

Figure 1 The portrait of Mathinna

> Mathinna was a Tasmanian Aboriginal child born in 1835 and taken from her family at age five by the Governor of Tasmania, John Franklin, and his wife Jane. It is said Mathinna arrived at Government House with a kangaroo skin, a rush basket, some shell necklaces and a pet possum. When the Franklins returned to England in 1843 they left her behind, and in the following years Mathinna struggled to find a sense of belonging in either black or white society. She died at age 17 as a result of alcohol abuse not long after the watershed events of the abolition of transportation, the granting of self-government and the official renaming to Tasmania.

Knowledge about texts and language

Choices for using 'Stolen Child: Mathinna's story' from *Australians all* (Wheatley & Searle, p93, 2013) have been based on close analysis (see Table 1) of the extract and its features and how language features serve to organise a text. The features also define a particular perspective by placing focus on certain participants at particular points across the text.

Table 1 Analysis of the text and features of 'Stolen child: Mathinna's story'	
Context	*Australians all* by Nadia Wheatley presents a number of stories from Australians spanning the time 'from the Ice Age to the Apology'. 'Stolen child: Mathinna's story' is one of these stories. The stories, illustrated by Ken Searle, will both entertain and inform young readers and can be seen as an introduction to the texts that will be explored in subject History. However most texts suitable for use with students in the primary years are usually focused on informing rather than analysing. For this reason it is vital to clearly identify the genre of the modelled reading text and also of the target text students are required to write. When this is done it is clear what support students might need to re-package the information they gather from the modelled text for use in the text they are attempting to compose.
Social purpose/genre	The text is an example of a biographical recount. Christie and Derewianka make the point that, 'while many of the biographies written for young children are simple recounts of events in the life of a famous person, the more mature biographies evaluate the significance of the person in terms of the values of the person's time and his/her enduring legacy.' (2008, p. 98)
Field (What is the subject matter?)	Most students at this stage of schooling will find this text easy to read and as it is also a short text it allows time during modelled reading to discuss the background events and context as Mathinna was living in Tasmania before that name had been given to it. This text recounts the events in Mathinna's very short and very sad life. She was not an orphan but she was taken from her mother and father, Wongerneep and Towterer and brought up by the Flinders Island schoolteacher until at the age of five when she was again removed by governor Franklin and his wife.
Tenor (Who is involved and what is the relationship?)	Recounting historical events will always involve taking a stance from which to recount events as the telling requires the evaluation of the behaviour of the participants and the significance of the events.
Mode (What is the channel of communication?)	The retelling is chronological and takes an authoritative tone as the events are revealed to the reader as a series of facts. The channel of communication is written and the author's use of the passive voice to foreground events rather than participants demonstrates the skill of the author in crafting a written text.
Stages and phases	The typical stages of a biographical recount include the Identification of person followed by episodes and often evaluation of the person. In the extracts in Table 2 the episodes consist of particular events which build up a picture of the experiences of the subject over time.

Understanding features of a modelled text

Analysis of the modelled text identifies features that can be used to develop teaching strategies to examine how the focus on participants unfolds across a text.

Cohesion of the text can be considered through examining the use of active and passive voice in the text. This provides a starting point for discussing the author's language choices and the perspective being developed through the focus on participants. An analysis of the focus developed in the text is shown in Table 2. In the table the following colour coding has been used to analyse the choices made by the writer:

verb groups/processes
noun groups/participants

Table 2 Analysis of text that shows the development of focus on participants

Examples from the text 'Stolen child: Mathinna's story'	Prompts to identify the purpose and use of passive or active voice in developing focus and perspective
However, two years before Mathinna's birth, her family and all the remaining members of their clan were taken from their traditional country and (were) relocated to Wybalenna, the Aboriginal mission on Flinders Island.	Who took the clan from their country? Who relocated the clan?
At a very young age, Mathinna herself was taken away, and (was) made to live with the island's schoolteacher.	Who took her away? Who made her live with the schoolteacher?
Over the next three years, Mathinna grew accustomed to the ways of the grand folk [who had adopted her].	Who adopted Mathinna? The grand folk
They abandoned Mathinna to the misery of the Orphan School in Hobart.	Who abandoned her? They
Note (were/was) has been ellipsed or left out.	

When looking at the first extract in Table 2 it becomes clear that identification of participants carrying out actions needs to be inferred by the reader. This is due to the use of passive voice where Mathinna, the one who is affected, is placed first in the clause. This obscures the doer of the action. In the second extract the people doing the action (the grandfolk) are placed earlier in the clause. This makes it clear as to who carried out the action. The use of the prompts in column 2 of Table 2 assists in developing inferential and literal comprehension related to the use of passive and active voice. 'If teachers make this use of the passive form of the verb explicit to students, this knowledge will help them develop critical literacy.' (Humphrey, Droga & Feez, 2012 p. 142)

Focus on language for creating cohesive texts

By looking at the modelled text the focus on active and passive voice can be used by the teacher to guide discussion about how meanings are woven throughout a text to develop a well-organised, cohesive text. Such choices are made based upon the mode or channel of communication appropriate for the context.

Along with other features like nominalisation; Theme of clause; sentence, paragraph and text openers (See Derewianka, 2011 and Humphrey, Droga & Feez, 2012), the use of passive and active voice can help to develop perspective and cohesion in a text.

Deconstructing the text during modelled reading will help students to identify the words and phrases that are used to position the reader or define a perspective. For instance the examples of the verbal groups in Table 2 can be used to identify the participants as doers of the actions. Some of these verbal groups are passive eg, *were taken* and (were) *relocated.* The passive voice, as opposed to the active voice does not put the actor clearly in the picture rather the action is the focus of the utterance. For instance:

> What happened to the window?
>
> Active voice: *John broke the window.* (Actor clearly identified)
>
> Passive voice: *The window was broken.* (Opportunity to omit actor)

> The passive form enables speakers and writers not only to change the theme of a clause, but also to 'ignore' and leave out the responsible participant altogether. (Humphrey, Droga & Feez, 2012, p. 142)

Consider the statements where the doers are identified and condemned as those who ***abandoned*** Mathinna. This could be very much softened or obscured by using the passive voice *Mathinna* ***was abandoned*** *to the misery of the Orphan School in Hobart.* So it is clear in her choice of the active voice that the author, Nadia Wheatley, wants the reader to understand who was responsible for Mathinna's misery.

In this text the passive voice is used to keep the focus on the main participants, Mathinna and her family. However the understanding of who had the power to take a child from her parents lies in the background knowledge that the reader brings to the text as it is not stated. This resource can also be used to remove 'doers' from a text to present a particular perspective, so the author's choice to use active or passive voice is a conscious decision which reflects their perspective in the recounting of events.

A discussion of the passive voice provides an entry into the discussion of Theme of clause or sentence opener. This important resource places the focus of the message at the beginning of the clause, sentence or paragraph and it is the openings of each of these aspects of the whole text which make it cohesive. This allows the author to focus the reader's attention. It is also through this resource that a perspective may be developed.

Nominalisation is another resource that allows the author to change verbs, conjunctions and adjectives to nouns in order to place them in this privileged place in the text as the openers of clauses, sentences and paragraphs.

For example:

From verb to noun: adopted → adoption

From conjunction to noun: because → the reason

From adjective to noun: miserable → misery

> Nominalisation is a language resource frequently found in written language whereby action-orientated processes (verb groups) are expressed as things or ideas (nouns in noun groups). (Derewianka & Jones, 2012, p. 25)

The sample joint construction of a newspaper article (Figure 2) gives some examples of how nominalisation and passive voice can be used in paragraph and sentence openers to develop a perspective.

In Figure 2, nominalisation is used in the sentence opener 'abandonment' to summarise the issue which is the focus of the jointly constructed newspaper article. This is followed by a series of arguments and the use of the passive voice 'was decided' is used to shift the responsibility for Mathinna's abandonment away from Lady Franklin. Similarly, the suggestion that the removal and relocation of Wongerneep and Towterer was illegal uses nominalisation to develop a sentence opener that is focused on the main participants. Finally a reinforcement of an appeal for action again uses nominalisation 'the adoption' and an extended noun group to summarise the issue in the sentence opener. The cohesion across this text clearly focuses the reader's attention on the issues presented from a particular perspective which are developed through the use of nominalisation, the passive voice and the careful choice of sentence and paragraph opener.

Figure 2
Example of a newspaper article showing joint construction using passive voice and nominalisation

The Examiner
1843

The abandonment of native children must stop!

The abandonment of native children must stop because children should never be abandoned by adults because they need to be looked after until they are old enough to look after themselves. My opinion is that native children must not be adopted or abandoned. Children should grow up with their families because it is best for them to have a family life. If you were at school and all your friends had families and you didn't wouldn't you feel left out?

It was decided that Lady Franklin should leave the colony as her husband had to go back to England but did that mean that she had to abandon the Aboriginal child, Mathinna to an orphanage? The removal and relocation of Wongerneep and Towterer was illegal and immoral they should have been returned to their traditional lands and then Mathinna could at least have returned to some family members on their own land.

There are so many reasons why native children should definitely be returned to their families. Many parents have faced the consequences of this. The adoption of native children by colonists must stop now!

Supporting students to master the use of the passive voice and nominalisation will help them to create cohesive texts which can be used for many purposes. These tools while useful in creating imaginative texts are critical in the creation of informative and especially persuasive texts in which the writer wishes to persuade the reader to take action or take up an opinion.

The *Australian Curriculum: English* identifies the following content in Year 6 which can be addressed based on teacher preparation and knowledge about texts and language. Although passive voice and nominalisation are not explicit in the primary years' content, teacher knowledge of these tools can be helpful in talking with students about how to organise their texts to convey and adjust their focus to make it more cohesive at all levels as the focus of a text is built up from clause, to sentence, to paragraph.

Language	Understand the uses of objective and subjective language and bias (ACELA1517)
	Understand that cohesive links can be made in texts by omitting or replacing words (ACELA1520)
Literature	Make connections between students' own experiences and those of characters and events represented in texts drawn from different historical, social and cultural contexts (ACELT1613)
Literacy	Plan, draft and publish imaginative, informative and persuasive texts, choosing and experimenting with text structures, language features, images and digital resources appropriate to purpose and audience (ACELY1714)

Supporting the learner

Based on teacher knowledge about text features and language, the following teaching and learning sequence (see Figure 3) outlines steps to support students in developing independent writing. The students are involved in writing a hortatory exposition in the form of a newspaper article written in 1833 conveying a perspective on the removal of Aboriginal children from their families. The focus on cohesive devices supports the cohesion and organisation of the text and the development of the writer's perspective.

Figure 3
Adapted teaching learning cycle with emphasis on independent construction

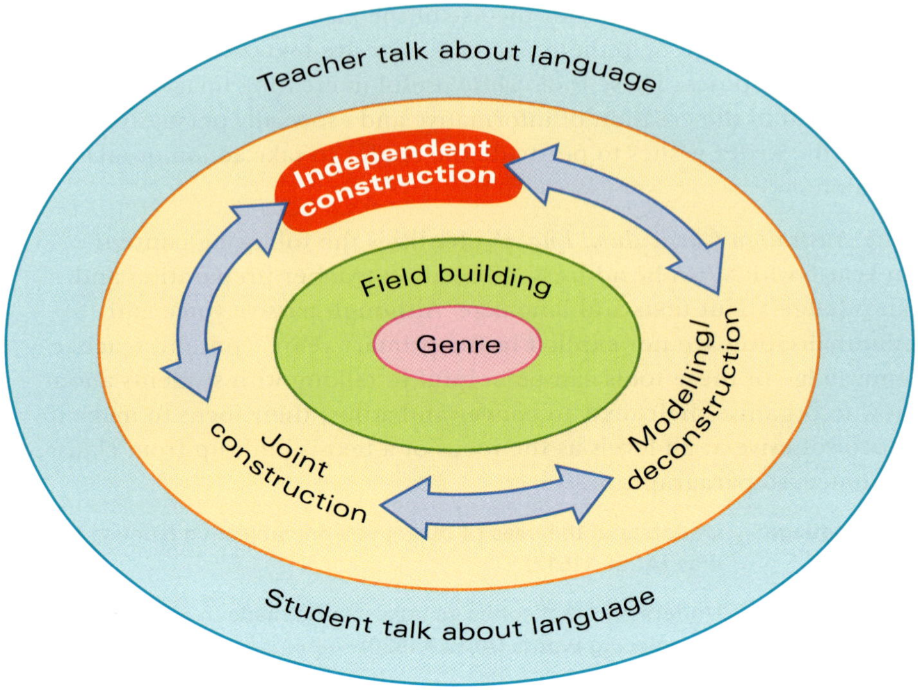

Prior to independent construction students should take part in much field building, as well as the deconstruction of historical texts and a joint construction of a text (see Figure 2 on page 132). During the joint construction, text structure should be reviewed and a topic sentence jointly constructed for each stage: Appeal for action, Series of arguments and suggested actions, Reinforcement of appeal for action (Humphrey, Droga & Feez, 2012, p. 192). Prior to and during joint and independent construction active and passive voice and nominalisation can be reviewed.

In the joint construction (see Figure 2) the development of perspective by carefully choosing the sentence opener, or Theme of clause to develop cohesion across the text can be demonstrated. Students have seen how the passive voice can be used to develop a perspective and focus the reader's attention and they can now examine how this works with the sentence opener 'the bit before the verb' in the first clause of the sentence. In this text the processes which relate to the participants can be nominalised and then used as sentence openers. For instance 'Mathinna was abandoned by Lady Franklin...' could be changed to 'The abandonment of Mathinna by Lady Franklin.' This is a subtle change but across the text the reader's focus can be changed from a focus on an individual person like Mathinna or Lady Franklin to more abstract themes like 'abandonment, removal, relocation, adoption' or 'separation'. This subtle shift at clause and sentence level can be built up across paragraphs and a whole text when developing a perspective.

Spotlight on language for independently creating cohesive texts

After the joint construction using the examples from the text as a starting point, pairs or small groups write a stage of an exposition focusing on the language features foregrounded in modelled reading and text deconstruction.

This statement can be used as a starting point for students to consider their stance on the issue.

> According to the *Colonial Times*, the practice of kidnapping only subsided in the early 1820's...Colonists stole native children for several reasons. Some entertained genuine, if misguided, civilising intentions. Not far beneath the philanthropic surface, however, was the need for labour. Many native children who were taken under the pretext of being 'civilised' became little more than slaves. (Clements, 2014, p. 22)

Tell students they are working for *The Examiner*, a Tasmanian owned and edited newspaper, based in the north at Launceston and established in 1842, the year before the Franklins left Hobart. Ask students to assume the role of a news reporter of the time that the Franklin's adoption and abandonment of Mathinna took place. It was at a time in the aftermath of the war which had only ended in 1831. 'The local newspapers discussed the need for a final solution, the editor of *The Tasmanian* declaring in February 1830 that "extermination seems to be the only remedy".' (Reynolds, 2013, p. 140)

Because they are writing as newspaper reporters from 1843, state that the exposition they will be writing may not accept the position of the 2008 and current Federal Governments that agree that the removal of Aboriginal children was unjust. Suggest that they might share the views of some people from that time and that hortatory expositions like this are appeals for action supported by arguments, for instance writing to the council to create a new crossing or park, or in this case calling for action relating to the removal of Aboriginal children from their families. This is unlike analytical expositions, which are to 'persuade the reader to *think* in a certain way by accepting a theory or position (eg. *that smoking is bad for your health*).' (Humphrey, Droga & Feez, 2012, p. 190)

The reporters are to write a newspaper story about Mathinna and the Franklins either supporting the fact that they returned to England without her or arguing against her *removal, adoption* and *abandonment.*

Suggest that the reporters have all just arrived in Hobart and are wanting to find out the truth about the Franklins and Mathinna. Use the drama activity, 'Conscience alley' (Ewing & Simons, 2004) to examine the issues related to Mathinna's placement in the orphanage. Call for six volunteers with an opinion of the course of action that should be taken regarding Mathinna and as a group ask them to each think of a reason to support it. Ask them to form two parallel lines (three people in each line) then ask for a volunteer to be the reporter. As the student taking on the character of the reporter walks between the two lines each person whispers their advice (loudly enough for the class to hear). When s/he has walked through ask her if she has changed her mind about Mathinna's abandonment/placement in the orphanage and what perspective they will take in writing their report for *The Examiner.* Support students to develop their opinions with questions such as: Should the Franklins have taken her with them? Should she be returned to her people? Were the Franklins motivated by kindness or selfishness? Should Mathinna have been removed from her family?

Before students write independently share and display the examples of how passive voice, nominalisation and sentence openers can be used to define a perspective. Then ask students to write a short article like the sample text or to choose one part of the text to focus on such as the opening statement or one of the arguments.

Students in pairs write one part of the text with a focus on defining their perspective. Support students by reminding them to use the resource of the sentence opener and the topic sentence. Encourage them to develop the topic sentence using the passive voice or nominalisation to focus attention on the participants or to conceal their undesirable actions.

Summary of a teaching and learning sequence

Field building

- Investigate the background events and context as Mathinna was living in Tasmania before that name had been given to it.
- Read the text and discuss the language used to define a perspective.
- Introduce a discussion of the Apology made in 2008 by the Prime Minister of the day, Kevin Rudd, (Wheatley, 2012, p. 250). Consider that this apology was given over 150 years after Mathinna was removed from her parents and how perspectives may have changed since then.

Text deconstruction

- Grammatical features are identified to develop understanding of how a perspective is developed at all levels across a text. Focus on the use of nominalisation and passive voice to support the selection of appropriate paragraph and sentence openers/ Theme of clause, 'the bit before the verb'.

Joint construction

- Jointly construct a newspaper report, which is a call to action to stop the adoption and abandonment of Aboriginal children. Write as a reporter of the time, in 1843, and focus on the use of language to develop a cohesive text from clause to paragraph, in particular, passive voice and nominalisation.

Independent construction

- Explain to students the difference between an analytical and a hortatory exposition and tell them that they will be writing a hortatory exposition because they will be trying to persuade their readers to act in a certain way. They will be writing as if they were contemporaries of Mathinna living in Tasmania over 150 years ago.
- Support students in developing a perspective by taking part in 'Conscience Alley'.
- Pairs or small groups write a stage of an exposition focusing on the language features foregrounded in modelled reading and text deconstruction.

Resources

Wheatley, N & Searle, K 2013, *Australians all*, Allen & Unwin, Crows Nest.

Appendix 1

Developing knowledge about texts and language across the grades

Year	Writing focus			Expressing and developing ideas	Language for interaction	Text structure and organization
	Imaginative	Informative	Persuasive			
1	Writing to engage an audience				Understand that there are different ways of asking for information, making offers and giving commands (ACELA1446) Explore different ways of expressing emotions, including verbal, visual, body language and facial expressions (ACELA1787)	
2			Writing to evaluate behaviour		Identify language that can be used for appreciating texts and the qualities of people and things (ACELA1462)	Understand that different types of texts have identifiable text structures and language features that help the text serve its purpose (ACELA1463)

Year	Writing focus			Expressing and developing ideas	Language for interaction	Text structure and organization
	Imaginative	Informative	Persuasive			
3		Writing to recount scientifically		Understand how different types of texts vary in use of language choices, depending on their purpose and context (for example, tense and types of sentences) (ACELA1478) Understand that verbs represent different processes, for example doing, thinking, saying, and relating and that these processes are anchored in time through tense (ACELA1482)		Understand how different types of texts vary in use of language choices, depending on their purpose and context (for example, tense and types of sentences) (ACELA1478)
3			Writing to persuade the community			Understand how different types of texts vary in use of language choices, depending on their purpose and context (for example, tense and types of sentences) (ACELA1478)
4	Writing to recount imaginatively			Understand that the meaning of sentences can be enriched through the use of noun groups/phrases and verb groups/phrases and prepositional phrases (ACELA1493) Understand how adverb groups/phrases and prepositional phrases work in different ways to provide circumstantial details about an activity (ACELA1495)		

4		Writing to compare entities				Understand how texts are made cohesive through the use of linking devices including pronoun reference and text connectives (ACELA1491)
5		Writing to recount historically		Understand how noun groups/ phrases and adjective groups/ phrases can be expanded in a variety of ways to provide a fuller description of the person, place, thing or idea (ACELA1508)	Understand that patterns of language interaction vary across social contexts and types of texts and that they help to signal social roles and relationships (ACELA1501)	
6	Writing to evoke feelings			Understand how ideas can be expanded and sharpened through careful choice of verbs, elaborated tenses and a range of adverb groups/phrases (ACELA1523)	Investigate how vocabulary choices, including evaluative language can express shades of meaning, feeling and opinion (ACELA1525)	
			Writing to define a perspective		Understand the uses of objective and subjective language and bias (ACELA1517)	Understand that cohesive links can be made in texts by omitting or replacing words (ACELA1520)

Appendix 2

Planning for teaching writing

Writing		Grade	
Reading			
Language	Language for ...		
Supporting the student			

Teaching context

Curriculum content

Knowledge about texts and language

Modelled text		
Text structure	**Phases**	**Text**

Text analysis	
Context	
Social purpose/ genre	
Field (What is the subject matter?)	
Tenor (Who is involved and what is the relationship?)	
Mode (What is the channel of communication?)	
Text structure and phases	

Focus on language for ...

Supporting the learner

Summary of a teaching and learning sequence
Building the field
Text deconstruction/modelled reading
Joint construction
Independent construction